THE
LIES
THAT
BIND

AND THE **TRUTH** THAT SETS YOU **FREE**

Dr. Deborah Waterbury

ISBN-13: 978-0998920887

ISBN-10: 0998920886

BISAC: Religion / Christian Life / Personal Growth

Library of Congress Control Number: 2017906017

Printed in the United States of America

The names of the people and places depicted in this book have been changed
to protect the innocent.

This book is
dedicated to

JEFF,

*the gravy on my
mashed potatoes.*

FOREWORD

Actually, this is more of a "fore-warning": everything you are about to read is true, and every bit of it came from my life. It's taken me a long time to be able to write a book remotely like The Lies that Bind, simply because it is such a raw and personal story. However, if there is one thing I've learned in the years now behind me in ministry, no one actually has a personal story. By that I mean that we seem to all share common threads of experiences, especially when it comes to identity and how that shapes our behavior and our choices. I've also learned that keeping your past safely hidden behind locked doors is not only self-destructive, but it is also utterly unhelpful. It won't help you, and it certainly won't help anyone else.

So after fifteen years, I'm finally ready to write this personal treatise, which doesn't mean I haven't revealed the contents of the next few pages in bits and pieces throughout my years of teaching and counseling and writing. But it wasn't until a good friend, who also happens to be my publicist, convinced me that I needed to share the complete story that I realized what a resource the information contained in the following pages could be for others.

Okay, "resource" is a benign word. This book is actually about deliverance. It's about breaking the chains and ropes that bind us, about discovering who we are and then living beautifully in the freedom of the truth. Far too many of us walk around in what I recently heard described as "grave clothes"—the garments of the dead. What a worthless endeavor! The children of God are the most alive of any people on earth, but we still put those tattered garments snugly around us, adding to the horrid ensemble at just about every turn. I did it for twenty-eight years, and I have to keep reminding myself even now what those grave clothes are so that I don't hang them back up in my closet.

Consequently, I offer you *The Lies that Bind* as an avenue toward healing. I have embellished nothing you will read, though I did change most of the names—you know, to protect the innocent and all of that. My words are all true, and most likely you will see yourself in more than a few pages. But keep reading. Although these grave clothes we manage to wear at times in our lives are ugly and difficult to remove, the robes of righteousness that are truly ours to wear are glorious, and they are readily available. I promise you that you will want to put them on, but you have to take the ugly garments off first.

Are you with me? I sure hope so, because freedom is waiting just around the corner.

ACKNOWLEDGMENTS

I would like to thank the following people, listed in no particular order, not only for their tireless work and unending dedication to the spread of the Gospel of Jesus Christ, but also for their seemingly bottomless patience with me:

– My husband, Jeff, who has stuck by me through thick and thin. Thirty-two years later, and you still make my heart sing.

– My boys, Spence and Miles. I know I didn't make life easy sometimes, but you two are my favorite creations. I'm so proud of you both.

– Kathy Cleary, for generously letting me stay in her townhouse in Silverthorne, Colorado, every time I need to write. Thanks, Kathy. It's now my "special writing place."

– The Board of Directors of LEM, for your unending dedication to our mission and to women all over the world. I love all of you!

– Gina Adams, of The Adams Group, for tirelessly making sure that everyone who could know about my books will know about my books.

– Martin Perez, of Merge Left Marketing, for believing in this little girl from Tennessee enough to work with me for four years and counting.

– Shevon Johnson, of Shevon Gallery of Designs, the most amazing graphic designer on the planet. Thank you, Shevon, for designing this cover and every cover I've ever needed.

– Brenda Woody, for simply always being there.

INTRODUCTION

Who are you? Have you really thought about that singular question? And I don't mean in any particularly existential way. I just mean, have you thought about what truly makes up all that you are—experiences, beliefs, attitudes, life choices—and then put those ideas together in a neat little bundle and said, "Oh, that's who I am"?

Most will probably say that they have. I know that I would have said that I had done that over the course of my life, but it wasn't until recently that I really looked at the answer to that question. And do you know what I found? The answer wasn't especially mind-boggling in its complexity; as a matter of fact, it was relatively simple. I've always thought that I was the sum of all the things I've done and all the things that have been done to me. What I believed was that every decision I had made, every step I'd taken in the course of my life was the result of other things I had done or other things that had been done to me.

Now, please don't misunderstand. I am certainly not relinquishing any responsibility for my decisions nor for my sins. Those choices were all mine, and the repercussions of those choices were all mine. However, I have come to realize that there is an important issue at stake here, an issue that, if left unaddressed, results in a life that is fully governed by the things I mentioned (one's attitudes, beliefs, experiences, and life choices). If we don't uncover the real issue, then each and every one of us will live this life based either on the things we have done or the things that have been done to us. And that goes for Christians, too. As a matter of fact, that statement might especially apply to the Christian because living life based on circumstances and consequences is unnecessary for those whose Lord is Jesus. Making decisions and living life this way is almost unavoidable for those who do not know Jesus. But for those of us who do, our identity lies somewhere else, and therefore our lives have the ability to reflect something far greater than just the things of this world.

Consequently, it's all about identity. Who are you really? Or maybe the better question is, who do you really believe yourself to be? My friends, the answer to this simple question will prove to be one of the most important conclusions you will ever come to. The answer to this question will be the determinant as to how you live and whether that life is one characterized by joy and peace or by pain and misery.

And do you know who else knows this is the case? Satan. Satan knows how important it is that we know who we are, and he has made it his business ever since man breathed to confuse us and lie to us about who we are. If he can bring evil and betrayal and sickness and sin and death into the lives of God's children, then he can assure that there will be accompanying confusion and despair. However, he is most ecstatic when the sadness over circumstances not only immobilizes us in the moment, but then also becomes the very fabric upon which we build our identities. His success in this area makes him drool in delight, rubbing his nasty claws together in utter satisfaction. Masking our identities in the things that happen to us or in the things that we do is the Devil's favorite deception when it comes to toying with the bride of Christ.

This tactic works because it's insidious. It starts when we are young because the level of confusion necessary to carry out this scheme has to be learned. Children are not born hopeless. They are not born into identity crisis. I was reading a book the other day called *Learned Optimism* by Martin Seligman. In this book, Mr. Seligman speaks of how each and every one of us was born optimistic. All of us are born sharing an untainted view of life and of the people in it. We trust. We love. We know joy. However, we are also born with a sin nature, so we are also born with the propensity toward hate and sin, but our *identities* are shaped by the world around us. Consequently, until that same world shows us otherwise, we are hopeful.

Seligman reports that this is the case until about the age of seven. As a matter of fact, studies show that no one under the age of seven has ever committed suicide. Homicide, yes, but not suicide. Why? It's simple really. A child who hasn't learned hopelessness can't maintain a level of depression long enough to consider ending his or her life. There is still hope because that child hasn't yet learned to be hopeless. A state of despair and hopelessness that can make a person contemplate suicide is a learned state, and it's learned by experiencing the horrors of what a person can do or what can be done to him or her.

Ultimately, it is in this learned hopelessness that identity is shaped, and the results are insidious. The shaping of our identity starts when we are young and builds over the years. It's so slow and progressive that more often than not we don't even know that we have built who we are on the premise of what we've done or on what has been done to us. We make decisions based on our identity. We live according to that identity. We marry and have children and build careers and love and hate and cry and laugh, all according to that identity.

And again, I stress that none of the confusion surrounding our identity makes us less culpable in the decisions we've made to sin or not to sin. We have been given the opportunity to choose, and even though we might be able to trace a choice back to something that happened to us when we were younger, we still choose to do or not to do whatever lies in front of us. Far too many psychiatrists' couches have become a place for free passes or self-exoneration. On the contrary, every choice you make is your choice. What I propose is that many, if not most, of us have been tricked into thinking we are someone we aren't so that making the wrong choices becomes far too much about mistaken identity than about mistakes in general.

We are bound by lies, lies about who we are and who God is and lies about what that means in our life. The lies aren't about our choices or even about the things that are done to us. Those are real. The lies are used to tie who we are to those things. The lies say that those things make us who we are. How many times have you heard someone say, "You are the sum of your life's experiences"? That sounds so logical, doesn't it? It even sounds intelligent. But for a Christian, that's the lie. You are not the sum of your experiences. You are the bride of Christ, the chosen child of God, the beloved one that Jesus willingly died for so that you might live with Him in eternity. That's who you are, and it's supremely sad that we make choices and decisions based on lies about our identities.

We are fallen, yes. We are sinful, yes. We don't deserve all that our Savior accomplished on our behalf, yes. We are nothing without Jesus, yes. But those things don't define us. Those are realities and truths, but who we are is identified by our relationship with Christ, the One whose propitiation resulted in our receiving His righteousness by imputation. My identity, your identity, is Jesus.

But that is exactly what Satan wants us to forget, and he has a fairly foolproof way of accomplishing that goal—life. He uses the very life we have been given as a means of keeping us bound in mistaken identities that are formed *by* that life instead of by the One who *gave* us that life.

The truth is that Jesus has given us eternity, and He has given us victory in this life over these kinds of lies. Satan's only defense against this kind of life-giving and life-saving power is to bind us in lies so that we don't live in truth. Jesus said in Matthew 12:29,

Or how can someone enter a strong man's house and plunder his goods, unless he first binds the strong man? Then indeed he may plunder his house.

In Christ, we are strong. Satan knows that, so the only way he can enter into our lives and truly mess things up is to bind us first. His binding material of choice is identity. If he can successfully confuse us about who we are, causing us to define ourselves in terms of sin, both those we commit and those that are committed against us, then he can make his way into our lives. He can't take our lives, as they are secured in eternity with Jesus, but he can make us immobile. He can make us unproductive. He can make us move through these lives as if we were something far less than we are, and there is very little attractive about that kind of life.

No one looks at the life of a bound person who lives as if she is the sum of her experiences and thinks, "I want that life. I want to be just like her." Not really. What's ultimately attractive to a dying world and the dying people living in that world is the life of royalty, true royalty. A person who lives in terms of who she really is instead of what she's done or what's been done to her, well, that's the sort of person about whom the world will sit up and take notice. They might not fully understand everything about that person, but they'll want what that person has.

Satan doesn't want that to happen. His only hope for keeping the people of the world for himself is if they see nothing particularly wonderful about believers in Christ. If we simply go limping through this existence, forever dodging bullets, shirking responsibility, and ducking under the weight of our own condemnation, then the Devil succeeds in keeping the world from wanting what we have—eternity in heaven. Instead, we look as pitiful as they do, and the job we are truly tasked with while living as pilgrims on this earth goes unfinished.

Jesus also said in Matthew 28:19-20,

Go therefore and make disciples of all nations, baptizing them in the name of the Father and of the Son and of the Holy Spirit, teaching them to observe all that I have commanded you. And behold, I am with you always, to the end of the age.

How in the world are we to complete the Great Commission if we don't even live knowing who we are? The answer is that we can't. We can try, and God is far more powerful than our shortcomings. He uses imperfect, confused people all of the time. He'll use us too, even if we can't break these chains that bind us. However, don't you want to be joyful in this life? Don't you want to really know who you are and live in terms of that truth? Aren't you sick and tired of being a pawn in the enemy's schemes, a pawn that he moves around willy-nilly whenever the mood strikes him? I know that I am, and I also know that the only way to really break those chains of bondage is to expose them for the lies that they are and then replace them with truth.

Exposing those lies is of paramount importance, and we are going to do that in the pages that follow, but we have to be very careful to fill the hole that this exposure leaves with truth. The emptiness must be replaced with something, and that something has to be the truth of Christ, the truth of who He made us to be when He died on the cross for us. In Matthew 12:43-45, Jesus was speaking with the Pharisees in the synagogue. They were trying to trap him in His words. He always spoke to them in parables, and in this one He was admonishing them about being filled with truth when the lies of the enemy have been extinguished. He said,

When the unclean spirit has gone out of a person, it passes through waterless places seeking rest, but finds none. Then it says, "I will return to my house from which I came." And when it comes, it finds the house empty, swept, and put in order. Then it goes and brings with it seven other spirits more evil than itself, and they enter and dwell there, and the last state of that person is worse than the first.

Roaches run when light shines on them. That's exactly what happens when we expose the lies Satan tells us, especially about our identities. Your identity is the very basis of your life. It determines what you say and how you act, in what ways you respond to situations and people, and how you plan what you are going to do. If you take away the lies that Satan has been telling you about your identity, a blank space will remain.

Have you ever been to the ocean and dug a hole in the sand when the tide was out, just to have that hole fill with water the minute the tide came back in? The water rushed in and filled the void left after you dug a hole that had once been filled with sand. In the same way, we must be careful not to let the world fill the hole left in our hearts once we've emptied them of the Devil's lies. Instead, we must fill those places with truth, living lives characterized by that truth in the victory that is truly ours. Let us fulfill the Great Commission in the beauty and strength of a free man, not as a man who is bound.

In the next few pages, I'm going to be more transparent than I have ever been about my own life and about the lies the enemy has told me about my identity. I do not do so in order to be a sensationalist or to intimate that my life is somehow different or more special than yours. And believe me, I certainly do not do so in order to portray myself as some sort of martyr. To the contrary, I speak of my life and the lies I've believed about my identity so that I can move you to the same truths I finally saw, thereby prayerfully moving you out of those horrible chains that now bind you. Only this realization can bring you into the freedom that comes from seeing the truth of who Christ died to make you.

I look back at the things I'm about to tell you almost in wonder. I know they happened, and I know I did them, but that life seems like it was lived by someone else. In some ways, that is true, but in more ways, it's not. I have been redeemed by my Savior and given the position as His beloved bride since the day I gave my life to him at the age of eleven. My position in Christ never changed. I just lived as if it had, and that remains a great sadness to me.

But no more will I live my life according to the great and terrible Deceiver; my life has changed. And it is time for you to live no more according to those same lies. Live as the cherished bride of the Most High. Walk in the joy known only to those who stand no more bound by lies but who walk in glorious truth.

And then let's go tell someone! Let's tell lots of "someones" about this beautiful, grace-filled, free, and joyful life.

May the Lord grant you discernment and patience in the days ahead, giving you true insight into the lies you may have believed and full acceptance of the truth of who you are. In Jesus' Name, I pray these things, Amen.

CONTENTS

CHAPTER ONE

LIE #1
"You Are Worthless"

"Don't Forget the Softball Game!"

"Go on home now, Debbie."

I was still lying on the couch, my jeans and underwear still bunched up at my ankles. Slowly, the hands that had been keeping my shoulders pinned to the scratchy tweed cushion released their hold. Within seconds, I was left alone there, as my would-be friends walked into the kitchen for something to eat. I was afraid to move. Confusion and loathing and pain were all I felt, and I wasn't sure what I was supposed to do.

"You still here?" asked the oldest boy as he came back into the living room with a half-eaten sandwich still in his hand. "I thought I told you to go home. We're done; can't you see that?"

His younger brother, who was the same age as me, walked in right after him. He took one look at me still lying exposed on the couch and burst out laughing. "You look stupid, Debbie!"

1

More laughter. "I mean, I wish you could see how stupid you look lying there with your stuff all hangin' out!"

It was then that I realized my panties were still down around my feet. Quickly I reached down, trying unsuccessfully to pull them up. In my haste to cover myself and stop looking "stupid," I couldn't seem to get them past my heels and then my knees. In the background, I could hear the younger brother still laughing at me as I struggled. I had never liked him much. He was always mean to me.

But the older brother was a different story. I was so confused about what he had done to me, how he was treating me. I'd always had a crush on him, kind of looked up to him more than all the other kids in the neighborhood. He was never particularly nice to me, but he was never unkind either. What had just happened that morning at their house was a mangled blur of confusion, and I still couldn't quite seem to get my panties back up.

"Let yourself out the back door," the older boy finally said as he made his way to the front door. "We got places to be."

The youngest followed closely behind him, still giggling at the trouble I was having getting dressed. He looked over his shoulder and said, "Don't forget we're playing softball this afternoon." And with that, they walked out, leaving me with the task of finally getting my jeans up after my undies finally slid into place.

It seemed deathly quiet. I just stood there as the mid-morning sun began streaming in past the dingy green curtains. The house was simple. There was nothing special about it. I'd been there a hundred times before, laughing with the brothers and some of the other kids in the neighborhood. We had all hung out together for years, playing softball or watching TV or just being kids. When I had come over that Saturday morning, I thought it was going to be like any other Saturday morning at the Tanner house.

I was wrong.

Even as an adult, I have a hard time remembering the details. I'm sure that's on purpose as far as my psyche is concerned. I remember that it started out innocently enough—goofing around, some harmless 12-year-old flirting. I don't remember exactly how I ended up on the couch, my arms held down over my head by one of the boys while the other perched himself on top of me. They were laughing. I think I was laughing too. At first.

When the one on top of me began undoing the snap on my jeans, I remember being confused. What were they doing? Why were they doing that? And then I kept waiting for them to stop. I was embarrassed, and I screamed for them to stop. But they just kept laughing, and they didn't stop.

It was over rather quickly. I stopped struggling when the older one, who was the first on top of me, finished. I remember that when they switched off so that the younger brother could have his turn, I didn't move. Holding my arms down for that second go around was a moot point, but the older boy held them down anyway. The laughing stopped at some point. I can't remember exactly when. Then it just became the thing that was happening, and I simply waited until they were done.

I was never afraid that they would hurt me physically, at least not beyond what they were already doing. Even now as I look back on it, I feel that things simply got out of hand for them, and they just didn't stop doing what their teenage hormones told them to do. I'm not excusing them, but I am explaining that I don't think they would have hit me or done anything worse.

I'm sure that neither one of them was a virgin going into that morning, and maybe they assumed that I wasn't either. I don't know. But what I do know is that the act itself would have certainly been enough to damage me psychologically, but I think what proved to be the defining point for me and how I would see myself for years afterward was their nonchalant behavior when they were done. They finished and went to get something to eat. Then they just told me to go home. They didn't tell me to keep quiet or threaten me in any way. As a matter of fact, the younger reminded me about the softball game later that day.

It was as if I had fulfilled my purpose and then was excused.

So I went home. My mom and dad were at work, and my younger sister and brother were watching TV or playing, but I remember just going upstairs and taking a shower. I didn't cry. I kept my mouth closed. I suppose what happened to me was very much like date rape, and I fully understand why most women who have been molested in this manner simply don't say anything. After all, the lack of violent behavior in the form of threats or physical harm after the rape happens is enough to throw the victim into serious confusion. Did I do something wrong that made them think they could do that? Was that my fault? Why didn't I fight? Why would he think he could do that? What will people think of me? And so, like a lot of those women, I simply never spoke of it.

I wouldn't speak of it again until my life was in utter shambles twenty-eight years later and it came out in a counseling session. Of course, my counselor and I then examined it in detail, and there was quite a lot of healing that took place simply from my talking about it. However, it wasn't until recently that what happened to me on my neighbors' couch some forty-two years ago finally clicked into place in terms of my total healing. I finally saw the truth of the identity lies I had believed for so many years and how those lies began that Saturday morning with two boys I thought were my friends. That lie began when I saw myself as a throwaway, a worthless thing to be used and tossed away when the other person was finished.

It didn't matter that I had given my life to Christ a year earlier. It didn't matter that my identity was secured that day in Smyrna, Tennessee, when I walked down the aisle at our family's home church, proclaimed that I was a sinner in need of God's grace, and accepted Jesus as my only Lord and Savior. None of that mattered the day I was introduced to the lie that in spite of the magnificent truth about who I was in Christ, now I was a worthless thing used for the pleasure of two boys. That day was the first day of a life of skewed identity, a falsehood that was initiated in my thinking on that Saturday morning, and I never realized it until about six weeks ago.

I've been in ministry now for about twelve years, and over the course of these years, I've written a lot of books, taught a lot of conferences, and counseled a lot of women, many of whom have a past scarred by molestation or some other form of abuse. Women, and men for that matter, will generally choose one of two courses for their lives after suffering some sort of sexual abuse when they are young. They will either become promiscuous or completely shut off in the area of sex. Commonly, promiscuity results from the sexual abuse, so my story really isn't much different from that of many others.

Sexual abuse causes the one abused to feel that control over what happens to them has been taken away. Consequently, using sex to feel a semblance of control later in life is very common. When the abuse comes at the hand of a loved one or a friend, then the issue is one of equating love and acceptance with the sexual act. Again, these are common responses to a horrible injustice, and talking about them is of paramount importance.

However, there are other far-reaching implications of such a devastating experience, and sexual, or any other kind of abuse for that matter, are not the only sources of identity confusion. All of us, Christians and non-Christians alike, have had things happen to us while we were young that begin the identity-definition process. Your defining moment might be in your relationship with a parent or sibling, or maybe it was dealing with the death or sickness of a loved one, or maybe it was framed by the words an adult used during your formative years. So many sins are committed against the young, and every single one of those sinful acts can and will in some way begin the process of our identifying who we are. Mine just happened to come at the hands of childhood friends on the couch in their parents' living room. Yours could have come from a myriad of other places. Though looking at those things and working through them is extremely important, what is probably even more important is identifying the lie you began to believe about yourself because of them.

This, I believe, is Satan's favorite of the lies he uses to bind God's children. It's the lie of worthlessness. It is the lie that says, "You aren't worth anything. You are nothing. You are less than nothing, and you will always be less than nothing. You are worthless."

THE THROWAWAY

For me, being sexually abused by friends when I was twelve, then nonchalantly told to go home, and then reminded that we had a softball game later that afternoon was all it took. I went home confused and hurt, but I also went home sure that I was nothing—a throwaway. I was nothing more than something to be used and then tossed to the side. And even though those were not the words used (truthfully, I've never had those words said to me), that's what I believed because that's what the evidence suggested. Some of you have actually endured the pain of hearing those words, and so, of course, you believed them. Everything about our lives begins to be formed by that untruth, and it is insidious.

For most of my life, I didn't think that event and its accompanying lie affected me. I went on with life. I did go play softball that afternoon. I did see those boys again and again, though at least I was wise enough never to go over to their house when I knew there weren't going to be loads of other kids there too. My life didn't end that Saturday morning, but it was transformed. I looked at myself differently. I never saw "pretty" or "funny" or "worthy." I saw "dirty" and "fat" and "stupid" for the next twenty-eight years. And whether I knew it or not, every decision I made from that day forward was a decision made based on that lie. Every step I took, every word I spoke, every single thing I did was done and said from that platform, and I didn't even know it.

I simply lived it.

There were so many men in the years that followed, even after I was married. Often they were one-night stands, but sometimes my time with them was longer. No matter who it was or how many times we were together though, the reasons were the same: I wanted to feel worthy and loved and adored. I wanted to matter, and I learned that sex was what I had to offer. The lie I believed was that there was nothing else about me that made me worth a person's time, so if I had to give sex so that I could feel important, then that's what I gave. Generally each of these men would throw me away when they were done, just like those boys had done, and occasionally I did the throwing away, but the end result was always the same. I was left with a gaping hole in my heart and no way to fill it.

A lot is sad about those attempts to find self-worth, but the saddest thing of all was that none of what I believed was true. Every time I had sex with another man or "conquered" him in this way, I was building on a lie that began years before, but none of my conquests erased what was true. Jesus took me as His when I was eleven, and not one sin I committed changed that beautiful fact. I simply wasn't living in the truth of what was. I was living in the lie the Deceiver had told me, and then I propagated the effects of that lie every time I succumbed to it.

You see, if the Devil can launch us into a downward spiral of mistaken

7

identity when we are young, which is almost always when he does it, then we will be hard-pressed to see the lie as we get older. Instead, we see the choices we make and the things that happen to us as either payment for our sin or validation of our negative thoughts. The repeated lies produce a vicious cycle and one that few escape. Yet, the escape hatch is readily available. Once we have secured our place in eternity by accepting perfect

and incomparable love from the Savior of the world, then the escape hatch is looking at that love for what it is. God is love, and He is right there. He never moves. He never leaves.

Satan knows that God's love is the way of escape, so his best weapon is to sidetrack us with lies about who we are.

Satan knows that God's love is the way of escape, so his best weapon is to sidetrack us with lies about who we are. Once he starts that cycle, our sin natures will take over, and the choices we make are nothing short of self-destructive. We choose what we choose because we believe the lie about who we are. But on the flip side, if we knew who we really were, we would be more likely to choose based on that truth.

The moral of the story is—know who you are! Even more importantly, know Whose you are! For example, let's say you were poor and destitute and had spent your life living in a cardboard box in New York City. You regularly ate from garbage cans, and many nights in the middle of winter, you thought you would surely freeze to death. When you were young, you had been put in one of those boxes and told to live there. You were told repeatedly that that was who you were. You began to make choices based on that identity. You scavenged and stole and went hungry. You never moved out of that realm of existence because that was who you were.

Suppose that a man came to you one day and said he was a lawyer who had been looking for you. This lawyer told you that you had been kidnapped as an infant from the king of a foreign land. This king had recently died, and his entire estate had been left to you, his only surviving heir. You find out that what you have been told about your identity all those years was a lie.

You are royalty!

Do you suppose that the sun would go down on that day before you left that cardboard box and found your true inheritance? Would you ever eat trash again or freeze again or sleep on the ground again? No, of course you wouldn't! The truth has been revealed about who you really are. The only thing that would satisfy you from that point forward would be to live in that truth.

It's virtually the same thing when we live in the refuse of false identity, which is exactly what the Devil wants us to do. When we accept Jesus as our Lord, the Bible tells us that His righteousness is imputed to us. That means it isn't just given to us; it becomes us. His righteousness is now our identity. Satan doesn't want you to know that. He wants you to believe his lies so that you will propagate those lies. We spread those lies by making choices based on those lies. Our choices are still our own, so we must take responsibility for them, but would we really choose to do or be something that isn't royal if we truly understood that we were royal?

Every time I had sex with another man and he threw me away afterward, the lie that I was nothing—a thing to be discarded when the user was finished—was validated. I didn't know that my false identity was being confirmed. I was simply choosing within that identity.

I remember that after my very last affair was made public, things took a definite turn. This final affair had lasted about two years. I was convinced I was in love with this man, and I thought he loved me in return. Now that the lies and the deception about my identity have been lifted, I can see that he never really did, but I thought so at the time. When his wife found an email he had written to me, the secrets were over. Within a matter of hours, his wife knew, my husband knew, and pretty much the entirety of the 7000-member church we attended knew. I realized I had lost everything, including my two small children, but I was willing to leave it all if I could just have this man, this "love of my life." That wasn't quite how things went, and just like that old country song says, now I thank God for unanswered prayers.

I learned a lot through that part of my life, but recently I came to an additional realization that bears telling now because it has to do with this first identity lie that began when I was twelve. This man panicked when the affair went public. His reputation was on the line, so he lied about most of what had taken place, pinning the blame on me and even telling a twisted version of the entire episode. Because he was a valued member of the church and always the really nice guy, people believed him. But that's not what sent me into a spiral of misery and pain. What sent me into despair and made me contemplate suicide was the fact that in twenty-four hours, he went from expressing undying love to me to denying that he had ever even liked me. And with that, he never spoke to me again.

I'm a relatively strong woman. I've built my life on not letting people hurt me (another reaction to Satan's lie), so it had always confounded me a bit that his reaction when the garbage hit the fan affected me so badly. When I say I spiraled, I mean I spiraled. I went into a depression that was dark. I was in despair, and even though I did love him, even that couldn't explain the depths of my pain in those months afterward. I could barely function, and my reaction confused me. The day I looked in the mirror and thought that I didn't deserve to live was the final straw. I had to find the answer to this level of pain, and I found it in my Savior. Although I did not understand what I was doing, I began to look at Him and not at the lie I had believed, and this is where my healing began.

However, it hasn't been until recently, as the Lord has been revealing much to me in the way of identity, that I've begun to see how the Devil has used false identity through the years to keep God's children in bondage. That's when I finally saw why this man's reaction devastated me so.

He threw me away.

When the chips were down and he was finished, he simply threw me away and never had another thing to do with me. He did what those boys had done and what so many other men had done, but this time I had been willing to risk everything on the chance that maybe, just maybe, I was worth something after all. When he left me at the drop of a hat, it was final validation that I truly was worthless, and that realization sent me into despair. I sank so low that I didn't see any way out of my pain. It seemed that my life was doomed to consist of day-after-day darkness. I saw absolutely no end in sight.

"I WILL NEVER LEAVE YOU"

But God wouldn't leave me there, and do you know why? It's the same reason He won't leave you there either. That's not who He is. He promised that He would never leave nor forsake me, and for my Savior, never leave means never leave. God was poised in those final days of my deception to show me the truest meaning of constancy and love, determined not by me and my behavior but by Himself and His character and perfection.

God showed me what "never leave" means through my children. They came home from school that next day after all hell had broken loose, and those two boys, eleven and fourteen at the time, sat on either side of me, wrapping me in their arms and saying over and over again, "Mommy, please don't leave us. Please stay with us." They knew the truth. They had heard it spoken, but they showed me a love that wanted me to stay.

God showed me what "never leave" means through one woman. We weren't even friends before this thing happened, but God placed it in her heart to reach out to me. No one else did. As a matter of fact, my head was placed on the chopping block pretty quickly. The way she tells it today, God simply told her to call me and to be the constant anchor for me in the coming months. That's exactly what she did, and what has resulted is one of the dearest friendships I have ever had from the most unlikely of beginnings. She stayed with me through thick and thin, and I'll love her always.

God showed me what "never leave" means through my husband. When this last affair became a public scandal rather than a private pain, Jeff and I had been married for seventeen years. It wasn't a good marriage. It was, in fact, a marriage in name only. We didn't talk; we didn't do anything together. We pretty much just shared a roof. But Jeff didn't leave me that day, and he didn't make me leave either, though he had every right to. Even he can't explain exactly why. He just says that he knew it was the right thing to do. As I write this, Jeff and I are getting ready to celebrate our thirty-second wedding anniversary, and I can say in all honesty and transparency that we are truly in love. It didn't happen overnight, and it's been a long, hard road, but for those who obediently move toward God, He is faithful in all of His promises. He is in the business of restoring all that the locusts have eaten and making glorious beauty from decaying ashes. My marriage is one of the truest testimonies to that fact.

THE DREAM

Most importantly, however, God showed me what "never leave" means through Himself. The despair I felt was almost palpable in those months following the public declaration that I was, in fact, Jezebel. There were days when breathing was a challenge, and after one of those days, I finally fell fitfully asleep after tossing and turning for hours. Then I had a dream in which I was standing on the porch of a large ranch house. As I stood in the doorway of the house, a slow procession of people passed in front of me. Among them was every single person I thought had loved me over the years. Relatives, friends, lovers, acquaintances—one by one, they passed by me, smiling sweetly and then disappearing from sight.

After what seemed like a very long time, the last person passed by, the man with whom I had had my final affair, and then I woke up. However, I didn't wake up as one might think after a dream like that. I had fallen asleep while crying again. I had been crying out to God about my life and the lack of love it held. Although I had stayed with my husband and was trying to make a go of things, we were both miserable. Love had long since left our marriage, so it felt more like we were just going through the motions. The idea that the rest of my life was destined to be lived in this loveless state had sent me into this most recent crying jag. Those were the complaints I had been making to God when I fell asleep. Naturally, I thought that seeing all those smiling faces would have caused me to wake feeling better, but they didn't. As a matter of fact, I woke up in more despair than I had been in when I fell asleep.

I yelled at God this time. "Are you kidding me? I ask You for comfort, and You give me a dream that's basically telling me that none of these people loved me the way I needed to be loved! Really?!"

I was incredulous. I cried and cried and eventually cried myself back to sleep. I dreamed again, but this time it was different. This time I was floating in what seemed like nothingness, but within this place I felt secure. I felt treasured and cared for and loved beyond measure. Within this more recent dream, I was lost in a sea of tranquility that is truly impossible in this life, but for the entirety of the time I was asleep, that is what I experienced. It was like being wrapped in the softest, warmest blanket you can imagine and knowing that you are safe, that you are loved, and that you are treasured. When I awoke the second time, I looked at the clock and realized I had been asleep for thirty minutes, but it was the most amazing thirty minutes I had ever experienced.

I cried out to God again, "That's what I want! That's how I want to feel! Please tell me how to feel that!"

And just as suddenly, my head was filled with these beautiful words: This is how I love you now, Debbie. This is how I've always loved you, will always love you. Look at Me.

THE TRUTH

And just like that, I knew. I knew that what I had been searching for my entire life was the One I'd had since the age of eleven. I simply had to look at Him. What I know now, after many, many years of studying and teaching and praying and writing, is that I couldn't see Him because I had believed the lie that He wasn't there to love me. I believed the lie that I was worthless, a lie that began that awful Saturday morning, and the accompanying lie that I had no choice but to accept my worthlessness, finding love and happiness wherever I could.

What I want each of you to understand right now is that if you have accepted Jesus as your Lord and Savior, then the truth I finally saw is true for you as well. You simply have to do what He told me to do: look at Him. But notice the active verb there—look. You must actively look at Him, and the place to look for Him is in His Word. Looking for Him requires wisdom, discernment, and effort on our part. Solomon wrote in Proverbs 2:1-5,

My son, if you receive my words and treasure up my commandments with you, making your ear attentive to wisdom and inclining your heart to understanding; yes, if you call out for insight and raise your voice for understanding, if you seek it like silver and search for it as for hidden treasures, then you will understand the fear of the LORD, and find the knowledge of God.

Satan will forever want you to believe whatever lies he's begun in your life. More than likely, those lies began in your younger years, but we settle in them. We become complacent in those deceptions, but if we want to finally be free in who we really are, then we must seek the truth. Move toward your Bridegroom right now, today. Stand against the schemes and the lies of the Devil that will keep you in bondage. Believe instead in the truth that you are God's beloved.

FREE

To the right is a prayer of
deliverance from the lie of
worthlessness, followed by
Scripture that speaks of the
truth of who you are and
how you are loved. Pray
these words to your Father,
to your Savior, to the God
who loves you now just
as He loved you from the
beginning. Your true identity
in Christ starts now.

My Father,

Thank You for exposing this lie. Thank You for loving me so much that today, right now, You are releasing me from the bondage of these lies that have kept me in chains for so long. You willingly gave Yourself so that I might live, and in that love I see that I am worthy. I am worthy not because of anything I have done or can do, but I am worthy because You chose me, and in that glorious truth, I am now worthy. I pray against the strongholds that this lie has placed on me. I pray for restored relationships and reconciliation that are only possible through You. I claim right now, in the name of Jesus my Savior, that I am the chosen bride of Christ, a ransomed soul bought with the price of redemption through the blood of my Redeemer, Jesus Christ, my Lord. There are no weapons that can form against me because You are all powerful and mightier than the Enemy. Thank you, Jesus, for declaring me altogether lovely in Your sight. You are glorious and mighty and loving.

In Jesus' Holy Name, I pray, Amen.

SCRIPTURES FOR MEDITATION

You are altogether beautiful, my love;
there is no flaw in you.
— Song of Solomon 4:7

I have loved you with an everlasting
love; Therefore I have drawn you
with loving kindness.
— Jeremiah 31:3

But God shows his love for us in that while
we were still sinners, Christ died for us.
— Romans 5:8

Who shall separate us from the love of
Christ? Shall tribulation, or distress, or
persecution, or famine, or nakedness, or
danger, or sword? No, in all these things we
are more than conquerors through him
who loved us. For I am sure that neither
death nor life, nor angels nor rulers, nor
things present nor things to come, nor
powers, nor height nor depth, nor anything
else in all creation, will be able to
separate us from the love of God in
Christ Jesus our Lord.
— Romans 8:35, 37-39

*But God, being rich in mercy, because of
the great love with which he loved us, even
when we were dead in our trespasses, made
us alive together with Christ.*
– Ephesians 2:4-5

*But when the goodness and loving
kindness of God our Savior appeared, he
saved us, not because of works done by us
in righteousness, but according to his own
mercy, by the washing of regeneration
and renewal of the Holy Spirit, whom he
poured out on us richly through
Jesus Christ our Savior.*
– Titus 3:4-6

*In this the love of God was made manifest
among us, that God sent his only Son
into the world, so that we might live
through him. In this is love, not that
we have loved God but that he loved us
and sent his Son to be the
propitiation for our sins.*
– 1 John 4:9-10

CHAPTER TWO

LIE #2
"Image is Everything"

"The Set Up"

The lunch bell had just rung, and we were all filing into the cafeteria. I hated this time of day. In class I could study and withdraw. I didn't have to talk to anyone. I could be a student and do my work. But lunch was different. You had to go into a room full of hormonal middle school girls and try not to look like you wanted to crawl under a rock.

This was the school year after that fateful Saturday morning in my neighbors' living room. I spent most days trying to blend in so that no one would notice me, but still moving through each day longing to be noticed. I was always a little on the chubby side, so I battled with self-image; my battle was not much different than the one faced by the majority of other girls my age. However, I was somewhat athletic, reasonably intelligent, and overall pretty funny. Those qualities usually landed me a place in Middle

School America where I could slide in relatively unnoticed at the "popular" table. The trick was to sit there but still fly under the radar because the one thing that every twelve-year-old girl learns quickly is that if you aren't *in* the popular group, you don't want to be singled out *by* the popular group.

One of my close friends, Julie, was a cheerleader, so sitting at the cheerleading table was a privilege I was granted because of our friendship. Lunch was over when the Tanner brothers decided to walk by our table. Those boys definitely weren't in the cheerleading "popular" group; they seemed to fit better in the "poor white trash" group. However, they were just cute enough and just rebellious enough that most cheerleaders gave them a *wouldn't-you-like-to-make-it-with-a-cheerleader* look whenever they passed. I'm guessing that's why they always walked past that table.

At just under five feet tall, I generally found it easy to disappear, but I made every effort at that moment to appear even smaller. My greatest fear during those days was that the Tanner boys would tell what had happened. It's not like I had a reputation to protect; the truth was that I was happy with no reputation at all. I simply wanted to be as unnoticed as possible because even though these girls allowed me to sit at their table and occasionally invited me to their parties, I knew these girls were vultures. They sat at that table every single day, looking for someone to devour. I remember watching a popular TV show some years back where one of the characters said, "Girls don't abuse each other like boys do. We don't hit and punch. We just tease someone until she develops an eating disorder." Those were the girls I sat with at lunch.

"Hey, Debbie! Whatcha up to, girl?" It was Mark, the younger of the two brothers.

Instantly, every single eye at that table was on me. I could feel the heat traveling up my stomach, flaming onto my neck, and landing on my chubby cheeks.

The boys had stopped at the table, and both were smirking at me. I

22

looked up sheepishly and said, "Nothing."

Then they began to laugh, and I thought I might throw up. The hateful laughter was the same as in that living room a few months before, and I sat there and waited for the bomb to drop.

"Come on, Mark," Tony, the oldest, said as he walked away. "See ya later, Debbie," he said slyly and winked as he walked away.

My face was so close to the table that I could smell old French fries and ketchup in the Formica. I could feel the other girls at the table looking at me now, including Julie who gasped. "Do you know those guys?" she asked.

I glanced sideways at her, trying desperately not to make eye contact with the rest of the table. "They live in my neighborhood, remember?"

"Oh yeah, that's right," she said before returning her attention to her tuna sandwich. Julie was satisfied with my response; there had been no malice in her questions, just curiosity. Not so with the rest of the table.

"So, Debbie, I have a question for you." It was Darlene. Of all the cheerleaders, I liked Darlene the least. She was tall, thin, and relatively pretty. She looked a lot older than the rest of us in the seventh grade, and she hung out with all the older girls. I never thought she was that great of a cheerleader, but she had the right family and the right look, and she knew how to use those two things to her advantage. She was also catty, so I cringed when she addressed me.

"I've been asking everyone this same question, and I'm curious about what you might say," she continued. She was sitting across the table from me, about three people down, and per usual, when Darlene spoke, every ear was listening. Consequently, an entire table of cheerleaders and football players were now looking at me. I didn't think it was physiologically possible for me to become any smaller, but I certainly tried.

Darlene leaned toward me conspiratorially and asked, "If you could be anyone in the world, who would you be?"

There. It seemed like such a simple question, even thought-provoking.

But it was Darlene who was asking, so I knew it was a set-up. They were all looking at me, waiting, expecting an answer, and I knew I had to give the right one. My mind raced, looking through files and files of possible answers in my brain. I wanted to say something genuine, like "I don't want to be like anyone else," but I figured the last thing she would want would be genuineness, so I tried to come up with something else.

My mind quickly landed on the face of another one of the cheerleaders who wasn't currently sitting at the table. She was in the eighth grade, and she was definitely the nicest of all of them. She was pretty and kind and always seemed to be doing good things for people. Surely she would be the right answer.

"I would like to be Candice Porter," I finally said. I looked around quickly, trying to gauge the response of the table. Everyone sort of looked satisfied and sat back in their seats. I didn't know how, but I had given the right answer! Thank God! Now maybe they would go back to talking about how they all hated the new skirts of their cheerleading outfits.

"Huh." It was Darlene again. I looked up sheepishly, but I knew what was coming even before it happened. It was, after all, a set-up. Darlene was going to come out on top. I knew that even when I gave what I thought was the answer they were looking for. "That's interesting, Debbie," she continued, "because I know that I don't want to be anyone but me. I'm happy with who I am."

There it was. She had done it—just like I knew she would. In one fell swoop, I looked like the insecure, sad, shallow little chubby girl at the end of the table. Darlene, on the other hand, was being congratulated and lauded for her wonderful answer, for her unceasing dedication to self-assured women everywhere.

Suddenly, every single person at the table was saying the same thing: "I just want to be me, too. Of course I don't want to be someone else. How sad to think you need to be someone besides who you are." Their words were joined by a chorus of "Yeahs" and "That's rights," peppered with an occasional disapproving look in my direction.

Even Julie joined the throng, "Why would you say something like that, Debbie? I don't want to be anyone else. Why do you want to be someone else?"

At that point I felt like I should defend my position, but it wasn't really my position. My actual thoughts were the same as Darlene's, but I had given them the answer I thought they wanted. I couldn't defend something I didn't believe. Instead I just gave in and admitted defeat. "I guess you're right," I said to Julie, and then I got up from the table. Lunchtime wasn't nearly over, so class wasn't due to start for another twenty minutes. It was against the rules to go out of the lunchroom until the bell rang for fourth period, so I went in the bathroom and hid in a stall until the bell rang.

Why hadn't I just gone with what I thought first? Why had I said something so stupid, like I want to be like Candice Porter? Once again, I didn't cry. As I sat on the toilet in the third stall of the restroom at Forest Hill Middle School, I didn't feel like crying. I was just tired and lonely and confused. I was done. Who was I supposed to be anyway? It seemed to me that if I wanted to be happy, then I needed an image. I needed to be someone. I decided right then and there that I was tired of being on the outside. I wanted to be on the inside, and for that reason, I needed to have an image.

What a big fat lie, right? But this world is built on that gargantuan lie. It's all about image. If you can create for yourself the right image, then you will be happy and accepted and a part of something. My twelve-year-old brain was ripe to believe the next lie about my identity: I needed to create a persona. I needed to be what people wanted me to be if I didn't want to endure the Darlenes of the world.

IMAGE BUILDING 101

And that's exactly what I did. After my seventh-grade school year was over, I went into my own sequestered state. I stopped talking to my friends. I didn't go over to the Tanners or hang out with any of the neighborhood kids. I started to exercise. I went on a crazy diet. I got my hair cut. I bought new clothes. I changed everything about me, looking desperately for my image.

In the fall when I went back to school for eighth grade, people definitely noticed. "You look great, Debbie" and "Wow, you've changed" were some of the things I heard. Boys looked at me differently. Even the girls looked at me differently. I walked with more confidence. No longer did I say, "Yes," to Anthony Perkins, who always wanted me to do his math homework for him. I proudly said, "No" when he asked, and I liked it when he sheepishly walked away. I remember the first lunch period in the new school year when I had the opportunity to walk right past the cheerleading table and sit at a table by myself. I wasn't alone long. It was like I was the new girl in school, and every boy wanted to sit by me. I relished the look on Darlene's face when her boyfriend, Charlie, chose to sit with me at lunch instead of her. I was on top of the world.

But the very best feeling I experienced during that brief period of "image euphoria" took place about two weeks after school started when the Tanner boys walked by me and my new friends on the school bus. Mark was habitually oblivious to everything around him, so he didn't even notice that he and his brother were coming close to where I was sitting. Tony, on the other hand, smiled deviously as he approached.

"Hey, Debbie," he purred in the most suggestive voice he could muster for a boy of fourteen. "Wanna come over later? We're gonna play some football and, well, do some other stuff." The innuendo practically dripped from his lips.

I didn't even look at Tony. I was sitting in an aisle seat, which consequently was next to the seat inhabited by Charlie, Darlene's former boyfriend and my new love interest, and I answered while looking out of the window. I could see out of the corner of my eye how Charlie was looking at Tony. He looked like he might kill the boy, and I loved that.

"Nah," I finally answered. "I'm busy, Tony. I'm probably gonna be busy forever. See ya."

Tony stood there incredulously for a few seconds before he heard Mark calling for him at the back of the bus.

"Who was that jerk?" Charlie asked after Tony walked away.

"Just somebody I used to know," I answered, but I couldn't stop smiling. For the first time in a very long time I felt like I had made it. I was happy. I was popular. I had a boyfriend— a football player boyfriend— and life was good. Happiness was all about image, or at least that's what I told myself.

The problem was that maintaining my image was a lot of work. Image, when you find one and then think that all of your happiness is bound up in it, becomes your number one priority, and everything you do is to maintain that image. I couldn't be "Debbie" anymore, at least not the Debbie I had been for the previous thirteen years. I had to find this new "Debbie" and maintain whoever that was.

And then there was another problem. This new persona was only known at Forest Hill Middle School. At church, where there was a whole different clique of popular and non-popular kids, I was still the outsider. No matter what I did, I just couldn't break through that barrier. Sure, when I became thinner and more confident, the boys at church paid more attention to me, but that's where my persona came up short. I couldn't break into their clique.

Of course, now I understand why. My church friends, though still hormonal young people, were Christians. It's human nature to have cliques, especially when you are young, but they shared something I had lost in the process of image-building. They shared a genuine relationship with the One whose image they now bore, Jesus Christ. Whereas I was His and would always be His, I had stopped looking at Him. I had left my Savior out of my image equation, and when push came to shove, any image I may have created outside of Him was always going to be false—and lots and lots of futile work.

I had left my Savior out of my image equation, and when push came to shove, any image I may have created outside of Him was always going to be false— and lots and lots of futile work.

The problem was that I liked my new image. I liked how it made me feel to have boys pay attention to me. I liked how it felt to have the upper hand on girls like Darlene. I liked many aspects of this new image, but I eventually found out that one image wasn't enough. What I eventually came to realize was that it wasn't necessarily the image that hooked me but the feeling I got when people liked me and paid attention to me. That little chubby girl who used to do anything she could to fly under the radar had ended up on a neighbor boy's couch while his brother held her down. I never wanted to be that girl again, and the fact that I couldn't break into every circle of people with only one image told me that I needed to become adept at having many images.

THE IMAGE CHAMELEON

I became an image chameleon. Some adults call it ball juggling or plate spinning. Regardless of what you call it, the lie about image—that what people thought of me could bring me ultimate happiness—started that eighth-grade year when I found out I could get the attention I thought I wanted if I became what I thought they wanted. If at school they wanted the cute, confident thin girl, then that's what I would give them. If at church they wanted that same cute, thin girl who also knew the language of Christianity, then that's what I would give them.

Once I got to college, I found I needed an entirely different image to fit in there. I joined a sorority, and they seemed to want the same physical image, but this image had to be okay with drinking and partying and, you guessed it, promiscuity. Unfortunately, lie built on lie, and the one I had come to believe that day after the Tanner boys had their way with me, the lie that sex was an avenue to love and acceptance, came into play at every sorority or fraternity party I attended. I had been able to go to college because of a full academic scholarship, so I now had one more image I needed to maintain, the smart girl.

At the ripe old age of nineteen, I learned that when I was in school, I had a studious image to uphold and grades to make so that I kept my scholarship. When I was home, I had the image of the "good daughter" to uphold, the daughter who never caused any trouble and always did what she was told. When I was at church, I knew what clothes to wear, what words to use, and how to behave so that no one would question the validity of my claim to be a part of that group. When I was with my sorority sisters, I had to be the cute, thin girl again—the one who had it all together, wore the right clothes, and had the right friends. When I went to fraternity parties with those same girls, I had to drink and blend in there, and if that meant I occasionally found myself in a compromising position with some frat boy, then I had an image to maintain there as well. And when I was with my boyfriend, Jeff, whom I married a few years later, I had to maintain the image of the good girlfriend, maneuvering that relationship and balancing it amidst all of the other ones.

Maintaining multiple images was utterly exhausting, but I obtained the one thing I thought I had always wanted. I was well liked and popular, no matter what circle I was in, and no one was the wiser—except me, of course, though I wouldn't necessarily describe me as wiser. Wisdom didn't come until much, much later when all of those plates came crashing down around me. All of those balls fell at once, and the color of my chameleon turned from vibrant orange to black, black, black. No, I certainly wasn't wise at that point, but I became really good at playing the game. I could balance more plates than a circus act, and the more plates I threw in, the better I got at it.

Once the affairs began, I simply got better at maintaining the multiple images. By then I had motherhood plates, teacher plates, and then the church plates grew their own plates. I had Bible study plates, small group leader plates, worship leader plates, counselor plates, and all the while I would throw in a man or two for good measure. I think I was still that thirteen-year-old who was completely convinced that if I could just find the right plate, I would be happy. If I could simply come upon the right image, the right man, the right look—whatever it was—if I could just find it, then that elusive thing called joy would also be there.

THE LITTLE BEE WHO COULDN'T

I remember one time when I was about twenty-one and already exhausted with my life, I made an appointment with my pastor. I was miserable. I thought if I could just express to him the depth of my misery without confessing anything specific, then surely he would be able to tell me what to do. If anyone had the answers, surely the pastor had them. I entered his office and sat in the chair opposite him with his massive oak desk separating us.

"Hello, Debbie," he began. He had known me for most of my life. As a matter of fact, he was getting ready to perform the ceremony for mine and Jeff's wedding in a few short months, so I'm sure he thought that the impending marriage was what I wanted to talk about. "What can I do for you today?"

I looked at my hands in my lap. I had absolutely no idea where I was going to start. I definitely wasn't going to tell him anything, not anything specific. I tried to think of the best way to describe the way I was feeling without really revealing anything. It took me a few minutes to start, and he waited patiently.

"Well, Pastor Andrews, uh, well, uh, I'm just so, um,"…the tears were welling up in my eyes…"well, I'm just so, um, I'm just so unhappy!" I couldn't hold it in any longer. I cried and cried. I cried like I hadn't cried in years, and Pastor Andrews did what any good pastor does: he handed me some Kleenex.

"Debbie, why don't you tell me why you are unhappy."

I almost laughed. Wasn't that just the million-dollar question! Why was I unhappy? I wanted *him* to tell *me* that and then to tell me what to do so that I could be happy. I blew my nose and searched for the right words, words that wouldn't tell him anything exactly but that might explain metaphorically how I felt. I was still set on keeping my church plate spinning. Finally I landed on the following metaphor.

"Well, I feel like a bee." I looked up to see if he was listening, and though he was looking at me, I'm not sure how much he was actually hearing. "I feel like I'm a bee, and I'm at the bottom of this large jar of honey. I can see the top of the honey, but I can't get to it. I try and try to swim to the top of the honey, but it's so thick and so gooey that I just can't get to the top. No matter how hard I try, I never seem to move."

There. I was actually quite proud of that analogy. It seemed to express exactly how I felt. Surely my pastor, this man who had known me for most of my life, could tell me what to do so that I could get out.

He got up and walked around the desk, put his hand on my shoulder, and said in all earnestness, "Debbie, everyone is nervous before they are about to get married. This is just pre-marital jitters. They'll pass; I promise." He handed me a book. "Here, read this. I think it might help."

I took the book out of his hands and looked at the title. I don't remember what the title was. I do remember that the cover had lots of flowers on it, and I think there was a young man and woman sharing an embrace. I stared blankly for a few seconds before he broke the awkward silence again while gently tugging on my elbow. Apparently, it was time for me to go.

"Now don't you worry your pretty little head about all of this, my girl. It will pass." And with a gentle nudge, I was standing outside of his office again, still holding that ridiculous book, while his secretary smiled benignly behind her own desk.

"How are your folks these days?" she asked as I absentmindedly made my way to the door.

I looked over my shoulder and mustered up the best church plate smile I could find. "They are well, Mrs. Kimble. I'll be sure to tell them you asked after them."

"You do that, sweetheart, and tell your mamma that I'm looking forward to the next church social and some more of that yummy peach cobbler she makes."

"Yes ma'am, I will. Good day." And I left, still the same bee swimming around in that same jar of honey. But now I was a bee who had given up. If image was what was expected of me, then image was what I would give. Nineteen years later, I found myself right in the middle of hundreds of broken plates, but the best part was that the jar of honey broke right along with them. I was still that silly little bee, and I was still floundering, but after years of image building and plate spinning, now I had to find out how to clean up so that I could fly again. I was making my way through broken shards of glass and a sticky, slimy mess that I had created, as broken as the plates around me, but now with only one image left—adulterer. Even from there, however, God was just about to teach that little bee who couldn't how to fly again.

SLOW AND STEADY LIE

Equally as insidious as the lie of worthlessness and coming from exactly the same source, the lie of image begins slowly. It will start at some point in your life, probably not with something monumental, but at some point where you allow the lie to take root. This is one of the top two lies Satan tricks us with because it falls beautifully in line with what the world portrays as truth. Look at the Hollywood tabloids. Watch and listen to celebrity or reality TV today. There are certain people in mainstream society who have made their entire fortune on image alone,

Equally as insidious as the lie of worthlessness and coming from exactly the same source, the lie of image begins slowly.

image they created and then propagated, image that the rest of society ate up in large spoonfuls. The world tells us that image is everything, and if you don't have one or the crowd you are with doesn't like the one you are presenting, then create a new one.

What the world doesn't tell you is the amount of work it takes to spin that many plates or juggle that many balls. What the world doesn't tell you is the complete devastation that will consume your life the minute one of those plates drops to the floor. Just as soon as one drops, believe me, they will all drop. You know what you're left with then? Exactly what you started with—you.

THE REAL IMAGE BEARER

Can you see how needless and insane the search for an image is for the one who knows Jesus as Lord? An "image bearer" according to Scripture is what a man and a woman are. We bear the image of God. We are to be like a mirror that is facing outward, but at a 45-degree angle. If we were a simple mirror that faces outward, then the world would just see us. But if that mirror is tilted at 45 degrees, it will reflect what is upward. That is the direction our mirrors should be tilted. What is to be reflected for the world to see isn't us or the images we create, but God and what His image will do for a world. On the converse of that, Jesus bore the penalty for our sins so that we can bear His image on our souls. If we would but see that the only image that will bring the joy and peace we seek is the one we already bear in Christ, then I dare say a lot of young men and women would enjoy better days in middle school, high school, college, marriage, and everywhere in between.

When all of the images I had created crashed down around me and the one I was left with was the one that bore evidence of my actions—the affair—, I finally gave up. I knew the life I had been living was over and that I couldn't hide anymore, but I want to confess something right here and now.

The morning after my last affair hit the airwaves (as it were), I remember sitting on my own living room couch waiting for my boys to come home from school. My husband was still at work, and I had already received dozens of condemning phone calls, calling me all manner of names. I'd just found out that the man with whom I had been having the affair was in the process of lying about most all of the circumstances and was consequently throwing me under the proverbial bus in every way imaginable. In one twenty-four-hour period, I had gone from plate-wielding guru to home-wrecking harlot extraordinaire, but sitting there alone on my couch, the only thing I felt was relief.

For the first time in what seemed like forever, I didn't have to lie. Everything was out in the open, so lying was out of the question. I didn't have to hide. I didn't have to put on a show or act in a certain way or smile when all I felt like doing was screaming. For the first time in my life, I was just me, and though nothing about me was particularly desirable, the relief I felt that the game was over was indescribable.

The work is done. There is no pressure to perform because the perfect work has already been done.

And that, my friends, is where God met me. You see, in every attempt I made at image-building, He always knew that eventually I would be without any image that mattered except for Him, and He met me in my emptiness. He met me with loving kindness, forbearance, and the love of a Father whose wayward child has come home. There was no condemnation and no accusation. There was only love.

Over the course of the next months and years, I came to see that image truly is everything, but only one image matters—Jesus Christ. I am His Image bearer, and I am made in His image. I want nothing more than to display to the world the love and identity of a Savior whose love is unchanging, unswerving, and never ending. And one of the most wonderful things about bearing His image is that it is so easy! As my beautiful African friend once said, "The work is done. There is no pressure to perform because the perfect work has already been done."

What image or images have you created over the course of your life? How many plates do you currently have spinning above your head? How many personae are you known to be?

My friend, if you are tired and worn out from the continual drudgery of being whoever the people around you need you to be, if you're exhausted from the constant pressure that the lie of image has placed on you, then listen to what your Savior says to you,

Come to me, all you who labor and are heavy laden, and I will give you rest. Take my yoke upon you, and learn from me, for I am gentle and humble in heart, and you will find rest for your souls. For my yoke is easy, and my burden is light (Matthew 11:28-30).

Lay down the burdens and cares of worldly image. Put them at the cross of Christ. Let Him be the only Image you display. Let His visage be the one that people identify when they look at you. I'm not going to lie to you; allowing His image to define you won't be easy. It's hard to stop relying on your image when the world tells you image is so important. If this lie didn't work so well, the Devil wouldn't use it so often. Expose the lie of image today. Shine the light of Jesus on that horrible lie and replace that empty place with the One who has never left you anyway. Lay them all down today.

GETTING
FREE

To the right is a prayer of deliverance against that lie that tells you to put yourself in the place of the one true Image. Pray this prayer of deliverance and meditate on the truth that will set you free, a truth that you are the image bearer of the Christ, the Lover of your soul and the One who died so that the freedom you long for will most assuredly be yours.

My Father,

You are glorious and mighty and worthy to be praised. Your face is altogether lovely, and Your countenance is one that brings life to the dead and joy to the downtrodden. My Jesus, I break today the bonds of the lie of image that I have born all of these years. Forgive me for trying to replace Your face with those that I've created. I declare right now, in the name of Jesus, that those chains are broken. The images of greed and lust and power and deceit are no more, in Jesus' name. I lay all of them down at the foot of the cross, and I take up the image of my Savior, the only one who rightfully has that place in my life. Jesus, let those around me see a difference starting today. Let them see the freedom I know now that I have laid aside those chains of image and instead move without hindrance in the love You have given me. Thank You, my Savior, my Lord, my one true Image.

In Jesus' Holy Name, I pray, Amen.

SCRIPTURES FOR MEDITATION

*And we all, with unveiled face, beholding
the glory of the Lord, are being
transformed into the same image from
one degree of glory to another. For this
comes from the Lord who is the Spirit.*
— 2 Corinthians 3:18

*But our citizenship is in heaven, and
from it we await a Savior, the Lord Jesus
Christ, who will transform our lowly
body to be like his glorious body, by the
power that enables him even to subject
all things to himself.*
— Philippians 3:20-21

*So God created man in his own image, in
the image of God he created him; male
and female he created them.*
— Genesis 1:27

The god of this world has blinded the minds of the unbelievers, to keep them from seeing the light of the gospel of the glory of Christ, who is the image of God. For what we proclaim is not ourselves, but Jesus Christ as Lord, with ourselves as your servants for Jesus' sake. For God, who said, "Let light shine out of darkness," has shone in our hearts to give the light of the knowledge of the glory of God in the face of Jesus Christ.

— 2 Corinthians 4:4-6

And we know that for those who love God all things work together for good, for those who are called according to his purpose. For those whom he foreknew he also predestined to be conformed to the image of his Son, in order that he might be the firstborn among many brothers. And those whom he predestined he also called, and those whom he called he also justified, and those whom he justified he also glorified.

— Romans 8:28-30

CHAPTER THREE

LIE #3

"Be Strong"

"She can do it? She does everything!"

"Church service starts in five minutes! Where's Gina?" It was Patty. She was the secretary at North Central Heights Baptist Church in Valdosta, Georgia, and per usual for Patty, she was running around like a chicken with its head cut off at 5:55 p.m. on a Wednesday night. I tried to duck behind one of the big white pillars in the foyer, but it was too late. She saw me.

"Debbie! Is that you, Debbie?"

I stepped sheepishly from behind the pillar and waved tentatively in her direction. "Hey, Patty. What's up?" Ha! I knew exactly what was up. Well, maybe not exactly, but I could guess. Someone hadn't shown up for something, and Patty was running around trying to fill absent shoes. I already drove the preschool van every day, taught the youth every Sunday morning, sang in the choir, and ran the new mothers' ministry. That particular

Wednesday evening, I had been at the church since 4:00 helping with Wednesday evening meal, something we did every week together as a congregation before services started at 6:00.

When we first started attending North Central Heights, I was eager to volunteer. I had one small baby, and everyone at the church was so helpful and nice. I loved Wednesday evening meals, too. We'd all get to church early and have a meal together, and then we'd all go into prayer service together. It was just like a big family. I missed family. My husband Jeff was in the Air Force, and we moved a lot. I missed having a church family and really feeling like I belonged somewhere. My battle with identity had continued to plague me, so when we made the move to Georgia, I thought I could start again. I was determined to do things right this time and to create the right persona. From what I could surmise, that "right" persona included volunteering every single time I was asked.

After living in Georgia and attending North Central Heights for a full year, I had begun to understand that old adage that says, "At least 95% of the work in a church is done by 10% of the people." The best I could tell, even those figures were too conservative. As a matter of fact, I felt like I was the only one who ever said yes to anything.

When Patty saw me peeking out from behind that pillar, I had just finished filling in for another woman who hadn't shown up to help with serving the Wednesday evening meal. Despite the fact that I had already filled in for that same woman for four weeks in a row, I had still agreed to serve the meal again. After all, I wasn't working at the time (unless you counted all the volunteer work), and serving was what it was all about, right?

"Debbie," Patty began as she ran toward me, "I'm so glad I saw you. Gina didn't show up for nursery. Do you think you could fill in?"

The truth was that I hadn't been to "big people's church" in weeks. Teaching the youth on Sunday mornings and then filling in for the nursery almost every week made attending an actual church service nearly impossible. In retrospect, I can see that I was drowning. I was drowning in the sea of an identity crisis, but I didn't realize it.

I was giving and giving from a well that had long since run dry. Jeff and I weren't doing well in the marriage department, and having a baby wasn't all it was cracked up to be, in my opinion. I wasn't sleeping, I barely had time to eat, and to make matters worse, those old feelings were coming back that maybe I had simply married the wrong man. Perhaps if I could find the right one, the one who would love me the way I thought I needed to be loved, then I could grab hold of that life raft and swim to shore.

"Sure, Patty. I'll do it," I answered softly.

"Oh, thanks, Deb! You are truly the best!" And with that, Patty was off trying to put out a dozen more blazing fires before the first song was sung.

I walked slowly over to the building where the nursery was located, next to the sanctuary. Jeff was flying that night, so once again it had been left up to me to get my baby ready for church, take care of his needs, and then head over to start serving the meal. Of course, the teenaged girl who was supposed to be watching my son came bursting into the kitchen about halfway through dinner, yelling something about an emergency. She dropped my son in his baby carrier at my feet and ran out. I found out later that the emergency was that she'd heard her best friend was out with her boyfriend.

My son started crying almost immediately, so I was left spooning spaghetti onto plate after plate while I rocked his carrier with my foot. And not once did someone offer to help me. I remember wondering why that was, but I was honestly too busy to give it much thought. Like any mother who learns to do twelve things at once, I set my mind to the tasks at hand and kept working.

45

My son had finally fallen asleep, so he was quiet for the walk over to the nursery. I was exhausted, and I was envious of all of the people I saw filing into church. I wanted to be in the service so badly, but I had told Patty I'd take the nursery, so take the nursery I did.

As it turned out, only one other baby was in the nursery that night. My son had remained asleep, but this other little man was a bit fussy. Eventually I turned off the lights in the little room and rocked him to sleep. In the dark and quiet of the room, I started to weep. I wept for myself and for my loneliness. I wept because it just seemed that no matter what I did, whether I was working hard at my Christian life or hard at any of my other lives, I simply couldn't fill the void.

I was weeping silently, so as not to wake up the little bundle in my arms, when I heard footsteps coming down the hall. I eventually heard the voices of two men, both of whom I recognized immediately. They were both elders, and they were discussing the upcoming festival sponsored by the church.

"Harry, we have absolutely no one to run the kitchen for the festival. I've asked, and no one can do it." Harry Cole was one of the nicest men I'd ever known, and he was walking with Jeremy Biggel, an equally nice man and a good friend of ours. Jeremy said the words that, unbeknownst to him, sent me right over the edge.

"Ask Deb Waterbury to do it. That's one strong woman. She does everything else. I'm sure she can manage this, too."

If it hadn't been for the sleeping angel in my arms, I would have screamed at the top of my lungs. What kind of lunatic says something like that? I do everything else, so ask me?! That made absolutely no sense! But do you know what? They did ask me—immediately after the service was over that night, just as the mother of my one charge was picking him up from the nursery. And I said I would do it. After all, I knew I was strong.

I had always been strong. I handled things. That's what I did, so I would handle this too.

It didn't matter that I was lonely. It didn't matter that I felt like the only thing I did was serve others. It didn't matter that my relationship with my husband was awful, that I felt like he took just as much advantage of me as everyone else did. None of that mattered because one of the many images I had created over the years was one of a strong woman. I prided myself on my strength, and the world told me that my strength made me worth something. So if all else failed, I would be strong.

THE INSIDIOUS STRENGTH IMAGE

When we had arrived in Georgia a year or so earlier, I decided, as I explained earlier, to create yet another image—one that was correct. I would be the good wife, the good mother, the good churchgoer, the good girl. I wouldn't look at other men or use them or be used by them anymore. I wouldn't drink or go to parties, cheat or lie, or do any of the other sinful things I had done over the years. I really and truly wanted to be the person I knew I should be.

Unfortunately, somewhere along the line, I made up my mind that I had to work at this new image, and I became convinced that my strength was my shield. I could hide behind my strength. No one would see inside because I had an armor-plated shield of woman power protecting me from prying eyes. I was determined to keep that shield up no matter what, and that determination held, even if I was really falling apart behind my armor.

Poor Jeff. He had no way of knowing what was really going on. He had his own issues that he was dealing with, and since all of us are by nature egocentric, I never took four minutes to consider that maybe he wasn't noticing my need for support because he had his own monumental need for support. It's a terrible cycle that ruins more than a few marriages. If it hadn't been for the fact that we were moving around so much and he was gone so much, all of this probably would have come to a head much sooner. As it was, however, we truly were ships passing in the night, and all the while we were passing each other, the chasm between us was growing larger and larger every day.

AND THE PLATE SPINNING CONTINUES

We stayed in Georgia for another six or eight months, and I never stopped saying yes to everything that was asked of me, I never stopped feeling used and taken advantage of, and I never felt the slightest bit better about anything, much less my image. Finally, one day one of the elders and I were alone working on a missions project when he looked at me just the way a married man shouldn't look at a woman he's not married to, and I grabbed the life preserver. Of course, I grabbed the wrong one, but I had been drowning for so long, and this "working at it" thing wasn't panning out the way I'd hoped. So in desperation, I grabbed the only lifeline I was offered.

That affair was short-lived since we relocated to the Philippines for another assignment shortly after it started, but the fire had been lit. I had an inkling again of what it felt like to be wanted by someone, to feel special and pretty and adored, and that was all it took. I picked up about fourteen more plates and started spinning them like an insane carnival worker.

The problem was that I never put down the Christian worker plate, even though I had picked up the "other woman" plate, along with a lot of other ones. I still spun that Christian plate as fast as all the others, so while in the Philippines, I had lots of images to maintain. Every one of those images centered on my self-sufficiency. People saw me as the woman who could do everything. I went back to work as a teacher, had another baby, sang in the choir, ran Vacation Bible School at a church off base, all while partying like there was no tomorrow.

The guys in Jeff's squadron began jokingly referring to him as "TDY Guy." In other words, he was always the first in line to volunteer for a TDY, which was a "tour of duty." He wanted to be gone as often as he could be gone, and who could blame him? I can only imagine how heartbreaking it was to live with me.

Unfortunately, the cycle continued. I was alone most all of the time, so when the washing machine broke, I fixed it. If there was a soccer game, I went to it. If the boys needed me to go to a parent-teacher conference, I went alone. I did it all, and I resented Jeff each and every time. The impression I presented to both him and everyone else around, however, was that I didn't need him. I didn't need anyone. I could use men if I needed the affirmation, and I could go home and take care of every household issue without them when it was necessary. All of this I did alone, and my strength became everything I stood upon.

All the while, the world told me my self-sufficiency was good. Strong women are the paragon of womanhood. Society frowns on the weak, and there is no frown as big as the one reserved for a weak, sniveling woman. I could be all things to all people, and I was determined to look good while I did it. Everything was about my strength. That was my new mantra, but you know what is true of strong women? They are lonely. I've never met a woman yet who seemed to have it all together who wasn't in reality crying out for someone to take care of her. However, a strong woman is not going to admit her need because to admit that is to admit weakness, and then who is she? The world will tell her she's nothing. I refused to be nothing, so instead I became everything to everyone.

The next five years were terrible. Jeff and I finished three years in the Philippines and went straight to England for two more years. I gave up at least one of my identity plates by the time we got to England. I grew tired of twirling that Christian plate, so I threw that one down. I decided to work instead on the plates of appearance again. Lots of crazy diets, tanning beds, and intoxicated British parties later, we were back to square one. Jeff found out about an affair I was having with a much younger British man, and once again, I was at a crossroads. Was I going to finally throw all of the plates down and run headlong into what I thought would bring me the happiness I wanted so badly, or was I going to remain the plate-twirling master of ceremonies?

To make a long story short, I didn't leave, at least not that time. I went back to Jeff, but I made it clear to him that I was only coming back for my boys. For reasons I truly can't fathom, that was enough for my husband, and we moved back to the United States, this time to Tennessee. This assignment had us the closest we had ever been to family, and it was a wonderful time of healing for me. After a long process, I repented of every one of my past sins—again— and determined that I was going to be the Christian woman I was supposed to be—again.

We were in Tennessee for two more years, and I did what I do best—I dove into service. I taught middle school and served tirelessly at church. Jeff and I mended the fences as best we could, thinking we were moving in the right direction. I really did feel like the worst was behind us, and I thought I really was on the path to happiness. Little did I realize that I hadn't stepped off of the path of trusting my own strength—the path I had been on in the first place. Sure, I wasn't being unfaithful, and I wasn't drinking or carousing, but I was still doing everything in my own strength. I was doing my thing, the "Debbie" thing, and the Debbie thing was all about being strong and self-sufficient. I handled things. I took care of Jeff and the boys and the church and my students and every single other task that was put in front of me, and I did it all because that's who I was. I was the strong one.

I'M LOSING IT!

It didn't take long, however, for the old bitterness to show its ugly head, and after a couple of years, I was right back where I started. I wasn't looking for another man, but I was looking for someone to see that I was drowning again. And when no one seemed to notice, I became bitter...again.

We moved to England a second time, and while I was a bit nervous at first about being there, God was faithful. I didn't contact the man for whom I had been willing to throw my life away some three years earlier, but what I did do was to immerse myself once again in service. By default, I found myself leading a Bible study for women, and it grew exponentially rather quickly. I was singing, teaching, leading studies, and taking care of two small boys, all while Jeff was away for almost the entire two years. The Bosnian Conflict was in full swing, and since Jeff was a fighter pilot, he had to enforce the no-fly zone on the Italian border. Consequently, I was practically a single mother.

I remember one afternoon after I had picked the boys up from school. I knew I had about one hour in which to feed them before soccer games and Bible study took over the rest of the day and evening. I was rushing and behind, as usual, so I decided to take the boys to the restaurant just outside of the commissary on base to get something to eat.

51

They were acting exactly as you would expect two young boys to act at 3:30 in the afternoon. They were happy to be out of school, looking forward to their soccer practice, and hungry. They were fussing and goofing around, and I was almost at my breaking point. Anyone with children has been there a time or two, so an explanation about how I was feeling at that moment is most likely unnecessary.

I had just gotten the boys seated at a booth in the café and sat down myself when a woman walked up to the table. As she approached, the boys had been busy slinging taco salad at each other, and I was trying unsuccessfully to eat while encouraging them to at least put something in their mouths. I was holding it together, but only barely. My head was a battle zone, and the expletives that I was uttering in silence to me, myself, and I were not something I can repeat in polite company.

When the woman reached the table, I recognized her as one of the newcomers to the ladies' Bible study I was currently leading at the base chapel every Tuesday morning. She said shyly, "Hi, Debbie. I'm sure you don't remember me, but I've been attending the study you've been teaching on Tuesday mornings. My name is Belle."

I couldn't for the life of me imagine what made this woman think this was an opportune time to stop for a chat, but I smiled sweetly and said, "Of course I remember you, Belle. You came with Adrianne, right?"

She smiled bigger when it seemed that I did, in fact, remember her. I hoped she would ask me whatever she needed to ask me and then continue on her way. The boys had now graduated from slinging taco salad to catapulting it from makeshift devices they'd created from spoons and paper plates. I'm pretty sure some of it had landed on the man seated behind us, and he was not happy about it.

"Well," she began, "I just wanted to ask you how you do it."

I cocked my head, not sure where she was going with this. "Excuse me?" I asked.

She started fidgeting a bit, switching from one foot to the other, and finally said, "I just wondered how you do it. I mean, I'm married, as you know, and I have two small children, too, but I'm about to lose my mind! But you, you always have everything together. You always look good, you're dressed well, you know just the right things to say and do, and you're even out for a meal by yourself with your children! It's just that, well, you're always so together. How do you do it?"

I sat staring at her incredulously. Was she out of her mind? How did I do it? I wasn't doing anything! As a matter of fact, I was losing it right then and there, but all of the raging emotions were safely hidden in my head. I was careful that no one—ever—saw anything except Deb Waterbury as calm, cool, collected, and in control. No wonder this young woman thought I had it all together. To be truthful, at that very moment I had to fight every urge not to smack the living daylights out of her! If one more piece of lettuce had flown across the table before she walked up, I might have lost it right there in the commissary café. And she was asking how I kept it together?

But I didn't say any of that to her. After all, I had the "strong" image to uphold, the one that I hung my hat on every day. So instead of issuing forth the string of expletives that was currently flowing through my head, I smiled and said, "God gives us strength, Belle. It's not me. It's my Father." I patted her hand and asked if she would like me to pray for her. Thankfully, she was in a hurry, so I didn't have to go through that particular charade. Instead, I quietly finished my salad, cleaned up what was left of my boys' ruined meals, and left.

Does any of that sound familiar? Have any of you left a situation where you know you portrayed the image of complete control, like you had it all together, when all the while you were absolutely losing it in your head? What makes us do that? What makes us behave as if nothing that's happening is more than we can handle? What makes us refuse help when it is offered or respond with, "Everything's great! How are you?" when asked if everything's okay?

I'll tell you what makes us do that. It's a world that's convinced us that being strong is the most important thing any person can be—man or woman. It's the lie that if we show that we actually need each other, we will be labeled as weak, and that is precisely where the Devil wants us.

JUST A BIT OF TRUTH AND A WHOLE LOT OF LIES

What happened the year after I was molested was just as much of a lie as when those boys defiled me that day on the couch. First, I believed the lie that I was worthless, and then I believed the lie that I needed an image, and then finally I believed that my strength must be the anchor upon which all of my images rested. The problem is that there is a modicum of truth in all of those lies, but only a modicum.

Strength is not a bad thing. It's just that the source of our strength cannot be ourselves. When we try and try to make our lives and the perceptions of others be about how strong we are, then the one thing we can be assured of is that we will become angry and bitter. Everyone, and I mean everyone, wants to be cared for, nurtured, and loved. However, the walls we build in strength not only shut us in, but they also shut others out.

Whatever the sin is that we are running from, once we begin to lose it behind those walls of strength we build, we will always revert back to those sins. It's simply our human reaction to our human attempt at solution.

I was drowning behind my wall of self-sufficiency, but I was drowning behind a wall I had meticulously built for myself. Then I got angry at Jeff for not scaling that wall to be my protector and nurturer. I responded to my anger and feelings of neglect by becoming more and more bitter, and before I knew it, all of my self-imposed strength bit me right in my proverbial rear end, and I sinned in exactly the same ways I had been trying to avoid. It's a vicious cycle, and all too many of us have willingly climbed onto that merry-go-round.

It doesn't have to be sex that we end up in. I've counseled many ladies, and it's just as often alcohol, drugs, or even compulsive shopping or stealing or gossiping or a myriad of other sins. Whatever the sin is that we are running from, once we begin to lose it behind those walls of strength we build, we will always revert back to those sins. It's simply our human reaction to our human attempt at solution. And that's the issue exactly. It's our human reaction to our human attempt at solution.

HUMAN SOLUTIONS FOR HUMAN SIN – FAIL!

The solution is never a human one. Yes, we are to be strong. Falling apart and screaming obscenities in a café when your children are just being children and you are simply fulfilling your role as mother is never the answer. However, trying to summon strength from within ourselves to combat that very human response will never work. Why does the world tell us to be strong and then not tell us what that actually means? Because the Devil is the lord of this earth, and he will do everything he can to keep the truth about strength elusive and unseen.

What eventually happened many years after this scene in England, years where my strength had been my anchor, was that my world came crashing down around me. My last affair was exposed in a very public way, as I have mentioned, but my initial response was to find a sort of "self solution," though it was guised as a sort of spiritual one. Once the affair was exposed and I had repented, I determined once again to be the good girl. This time, however, I decided that my strength was the problem. I figured that maybe if I changed who I was entirely then I would be okay.

Identity again.

Me again.

I looked around at all of the wives and mothers who were lauded as the proper kinds of wives and mothers, and they all seemed to be demure and quiet, submissive and obedient, which were all of the things I'd worked my whole life not to be. So I decided to change. I would become like those women.

For some reason or another, I equated the proper woman as quiet with no make-up and simple hair. Unfortunately, I was also raised in the South, and no good Southern woman left the house without her hair and face complete. That meant I was left with a bit of a dilemma. Since my plan was to be the opposite of who I had been and yet I had been raised to never leave the house without my hair and make-up "done," as Mama would say, this was going to have to be drastic. I was going to have to do this right. I went to Walmart and bought two track suits, something that had never before found their way into my closet. I cooked and cleaned and didn't argue or talk loudly. I kept my opinions to myself and did everything I thought a woman of this kind would do. That meant no make-up and no blow dryer. I was in a Southern woman's hell.

After a month or so of that behavior, to say I was miserable would have been an understatement. Jeff and I were actively working on our marriage, and I was spending every moment possible reacquainting myself with this God who had taken me as His twenty-eight years before. All of that was good, but I was completely miserable in this new skin I was wearing.

"I LOVE WHO YOU ARE"

One morning during my quiet time with God, before the boys or Jeff had gotten up, I was downstairs crying out to Him about how unhappy I was. I hated those blasted track suits. I missed my make-up and my blow dryer. I couldn't stand going to small group or Sunday school and not expressing my opinion, not sharing what I was learning. I was crying and pleading with God to help me be okay with this new Debbie when I heard Him say very clearly, "My Debbie, I love you. I created you, and I created your personality. It was my will that you were born where you were born and learned what you learned. I love everything about you. It's okay for you to be loud and obnoxious. Just be loud and obnoxious for Me."

I fell to my knees, weeping in joy and thanksgiving for those words. They were words of freedom, but they were also words that spoke to my desire to be strong. I am strong. I have a strong personality. However, what God made clear to me that day was that my strength was to come from Him, not from me. He wanted me to display for the world the woman He had created me to be and the strength He had allowed me to possess. That strength, however, had to come from His love, His protection, and His will. I needed to know Him and understand Him so that I could truly live by what Paul wrote in 2 Corinthians 12:9,

But he said to me, "My grace is sufficient for you, for my power is made perfect in weakness." Therefore I will boast all the more gladly of my weaknesses, so that the power of Christ may rest upon me.

We can't know the glorious truth of God's sufficient grace and strength in our human natures, and the world will certainly never tell us this. The only place where you and I can gather truths about strength and how to have it is

It ended because I finally bowed on my knees in front of the One who chose me from before the foundation of time to be His forever and I let His strength be my shield.

in God's Word. He did not create you and me to be doormats, but He also didn't create us to stand in our own strength. In our strength, we will surely fall. If there's anyone in the world who has proven that fact, it is me. Every single attempt I have made over the course of my life to rise above my circumstances, my feelings, or my pain has resulted in a crashing defeat. But that ended after this final fall, and it didn't end because I figured out anything terribly complicated. It ended because I finally bowed on my knees in front of the One who chose me from before the foundation of time to be His forever and I let His strength be my shield.

Furthermore, I no longer hide behind that shield, even though that shield is Christ. Instead, I am protected by that shield. There is a difference in the nuance of those two concepts. One binds you, and the other sets you free. Christ is my Rock and my Deliverer, my Fortress and my Protector. Once I realized I had all of that in the Maker of the universe, I no longer looked to other men or even to my sweet husband to be those things for me. No man is capable of being what Christ alone can provide. Once I settled in the truth of who I really was, it freed Jeff up to be for me what he could be, and that made all the difference in the world.

GRAVY ON MY MASHED POTATOES

There is an old saying that something is the icing on the cake when it's the finishing touch. In the South, we have a slightly different saying, which means something a little more fitting in this situation. When we have everything we need and then someone gives us that little extra to make it more wonderful, we call that "gravy," like the wonderful gravy only Southerners know how to make. Gravy can go on anything and make it better. When I've talked about how I feel about my husband now, I often call him my "gravy." He's that wonderful gift that God gave me that sits scrumptiously on top of the needs that are now filled in Christ. Jeff is gravy on God's mashed potatoes, and I love everything about that gravy. That gravy makes my life satisfying and beautiful, and it has brought freedom to a broken marriage.

Have you believed the lie about your identity that says you have to be strong in this world to be worth anything? Are you going through your life much like I did for all those years, bitterly hiding behind that massive wall of strength you've built, resenting every single person who expects you to be what you've painstakingly proven to them you are? My friends, I'm pleading with you right now to lay that all down. Break that chain that has bound your heart for so long and rest in the truth of Whose strength is yours to wear. He is constant, and He has never left you.

GETTING
FREE

Pray the prayer to the right
if you wish deliverance from
this lie that binds God's
children in unwarranted pain.
Let the wall down behind
which you have drowned for
far too long and step into the
freedom that exists behind
His shield, and then meditate
on His Word, a Word that
will truly set you free.

My Father,

*You are strong and mighty, a strong tower in times
of trouble. Thank You for Your constant character,
Your unwavering love, and Your generous protection.
Forgive me, Jesus, for trying to be what only You can
be in my life. Forgive me for thinking that my strength
lies in my power and my will. I know that You are the
only source of my strength and that You are the only
One who can protect and shield me in freedom. I break
the bonds right now, in the name of Jesus Christ, that
have held me in captivity to these thoughts. I shatter
the stronghold in Your name that has held me in
bondage to these lies, and I replace these untruths with
the truths of who You are and what You do for me.
You are my God, my Savior, my Bridegroom, and my
strong Protector. I stand confidently behind Your shield,
and I stand in the freedom of one who knows
she is loved beyond measure. Thank you, Jesus,
for loving me and for never leaving me
nor forsaking me, even in my darkest moments.
I love you and I receive Your strength.*

In Jesus' Holy Name, I pray, Amen.

SCRIPTURES FOR MEDITATION

I love you, O LORD, my strength.
The LORD is my rock and my fortress and
my deliverer, my God, my rock, in whom I
take refuge, my shield, and the horn of my
salvation, my stronghold.
– Psalm 18:1-2

The salvation of the righteous is from the
LORD; he is their stronghold in the time of
trouble. The LORD helps them and delivers
them; he delivers them from the wicked and
saves them, because they take refuge in him.
– Psalm 37:39-40

Whom have I in heaven but you? And there is
nothing on earth that I desire besides you. My
flesh and my heart may fail, but God is the
strength of my heart and my portion forever.
– Psalm 73:25-26

Trust in the LORD forever, for the
LORD God is an everlasting rock.
– Isaiah 26:4

Do not be anxious about anything, but in everything by prayer and supplication with thanksgiving let your requests be made known to God. And the peace of God, which surpasses all understanding, will guard your hearts and your minds in Christ Jesus.
– Philippians 4:6-7

Keep your life free from the love of money, and be content with what you have, for he has said, "I will never leave you nor forsake you." So we can confidently say, "The Lord is my helper; I will not fear; what can man do to me?"
– Hebrews 13:5-6

Humble yourselves, therefore, under the mighty hand of God so that at the proper time he may exalt you, casting all your anxieties on him, because he cares for you.
– 1 Peter 5:6-7

LIE #4

"You Deserve This"

"Judgment Day"

The hall in the church office building seemed longer than I remembered. Darker, too. I hadn't been back to Forest Grove Church since the affair had surfaced. Once Jeff and I started talking again, we thought we would find a new church. We tried a few, but nothing clicked. In the meantime, it had been made clear that I wasn't welcome back at Forest Grove. Apparently, the man with whom I had been having the affair and his wife had returned within a week or so, and the elders and pastors thought it best if I stayed away for the time being.

That was okay with me. It was a mega church, with over seven thousand members, and both he and I had been very visible on stage as part of the worship team. Besides that leadership role, Jeff and I had led a very large Sunday school class for a few years, so to tell you the truth, I was in no hurry to go back there.

I was truly broken, but this time I was broken before the Lord, which is exactly where I needed to be. However, the Enemy wasn't content with my brokenness. No, sir. Even in the midst of the baby steps of healing I was taking during those first few months, Satan never stopped lying to me and trying to keep me bound by those lies. His favorite lie, once I was moving in the right direction, was that I deserved every single thing that was happening to me. Every phone call, every unkind word, every horrible email—I deserved them and should take them with my mouth shut, with my hand out to receive them, and with the attitude of "Thank you, sir. May I have some more?"

You see, I was keeping my mouth shut, and rightfully so, but because God had told me to. Defending myself was completely out of the question. There was nothing to defend. I was guilty. It didn't matter what anyone said or did. My Father made it clear that I had one role in this newly found freedom once the plates came crashing down and this little honey-covered bee had finally broken free from the jar of honey that had been her prison for so long—confession and then silence. Any sort of defense in the face of such betrayal was not only horrific, it was out of the question. The problem was that Satan knew this, too, and he was certainly going to capitalize on my silence and my vulnerability in that silence. However, I quickly turned that silence into a "payment ritual" instead of a means of honest confession and nothing more.

What Satan likes to do so that we buy his lies hook, line, and sinker is to take a biblical truth, tweak it just a hair, and then present it to us on shining platters of so-called justice.

Satan is good at his lies. You see, generally he doesn't come at us with bold and blatant untruths. In the case of most believers, they would likely see through those kinds of blatant untruths rather quickly. On the contrary, what Satan likes to do so that we buy his lies hook, line, and sinker is to take a biblical truth, tweak it just a hair, and then present it to us on shining platters of so-called justice. The biblical truth in this situation is that without Christ, we all deserve not only every horrible thing imaginable, but also hell. We have no redeeming qualities in and of ourselves. Without Christ, we deserve hell. The key phrase here, however, is "without Christ." That's the part Satan likes to leave out. Consequently, when I was finally on my face before God, once and for all faced with the horror of who I'd become and what I had done, it seemed logical and even biblical that I deserved the condemnation I was receiving from every corner imaginable.

When the phone rang and another angry parishioner was on the line demanding an explanation and then expecting me to listen attentively as he or she told me exactly what they thought, I would listen quietly. Then I'd apologize and ask for forgiveness, and if forgiveness wasn't offered, I'd hang up with the knowledge that I deserved whatever I was getting.

When men and women whom I had considered to be very close friends told me that they did not want to talk to me and that I was never to contact them again, I obliged because I felt I deserved their wrath.

When I heard through the grapevine the ugly rumors that were spreading like wildfire at church about all the horrible and despicable things I had supposedly done, knowing that 99% of those rumors were untrue, I didn't defend myself because I believed I deserved their vicious words.

I finally saw the horror of what I had become, and upon facing that woman in the mirror, I thought, *You deserve every awful thing that is about to come your way. Shut up and take your medicine.* So I did. My pride railed against what I saw in the mirror, that woman who was taking a beating at every turn. The part of me who demanded justice and fought for it as often as she could was sickened by the woman I had become. But when Satan reminded me of the truth that I deserved God's wrath and left out the part of who I really was, I believed him and became the punching bag of condemnation that I thought I deserved to be.

About three months after the affair went public, Jeff and I were finally granted a meeting with one of the elders to discuss whether or not I would be allowed to return to church. The other couple had returned within a couple of weeks, but until notified otherwise, I would need to stay away, though I was instructed to enter counseling at the Pastoral Care Center. I went to the counseling sessions because once again, I knew I deserved what I saw as punishment. As it turned out, I stayed in counseling with the wonderful woman at this facility for eighteen months, and it was one of the best things I ever did. God is good all of the time, isn't He?

Anyway, the day came for Jeff and me to meet with Greg Thomas, one of the ten or so pastors at Forest Grove Church. On that Tuesday afternoon as we walked down the hallway of the office complex, I felt like I had a red neon "A" emblazoned on my chest with a great big spot light blazing on me as I walked. It seemed like a loud speaker was announcing, "Harlot in the house! Harlot in the house!" I truly thought I might be sick before we finally made it to the pastor's office door.

Jeff knocked on the door that was already ajar, and a kind voice said, "Come in, Jeff." Then he looked at me and nodded, "Debbie."

We walked in and sat on the two chairs opposite his desk. I was sweating profusely and determined not to say a word. He and Jeff went through a series of small talk topics, dancing around the elephant in the room for about five minutes. Since I knew I was the elephant, I longed for them to just look at me and finish dispensing whatever punishment was in store. Finally Greg got on with it.

"Well, I guess we all know why we are here. Debbie," he said as he turned his attention to me. "We, as pastors, are happy to hear that you have begun and are continuing your counseling sessions with Margorie. We believe those appointments will be beneficial in your spiritual healing."

I wanted to ask him why none of the other pastors had been willing to meet with me before now, but I just kept my head down instead, saying nothing.

He continued. "There was a meeting last night of all of the elders and pastors here at Forest Grove to discuss the course of action we are going to require of you if you plan to continue attending church here." He stopped for a second and looked at me with compassion. "And we want you to, Debbie. Please don't misunderstand our intentions. We simply want to be sure that we are caring for everyone involved. This has been a very difficult and very public trial for the church, and for all of you, and we know it is our responsibility to protect the body."

I looked at him and smiled sheepishly. Jeff never took his eyes off the floor.

Greg went on. "So, we came to an agreement about how to proceed." He pushed a piece of paper across the desk toward me and Jeff, placing it between us so that we could both see. "You'll see outlined here the stipulations for your return." He pointed at the first bullet and continued downward to each succeeding one as he explained. "First, you may only attend second service on Sunday morning. Second, you will need to park in this area of the parking lot," he continued as he pointed to a map of the church and its subsequent parking areas, "in the southwest corner. Third, please always use the main entrance into the sanctuary, the one that opens to the east side of the campus. Fourth, you are to sit in the balcony on the south side of the sanctuary, and finally, we are asking you not to go into the food court for any reason. We are asking that you come to the service and then leave by way of the same entrance that you came in."

I was speechless. I stared at the piece of paper in front of me as everything inside me wanted to scream. But I didn't say anything. I just sat in silence and stared at the paper.

Now let me pause here for just a moment. I want to reiterate that I do not want to represent myself as some sort of martyr in this case. I chose

69

this sin. The responsibility of the sin is mine and the repercussions of it are mine. No one ever made me do anything. Additionally, the church had a responsibility to remove both of us from ministry for an extended period of time once this very grievous sin was exposed. I do not now nor did I ever question the validity nor the necessity of church discipline in my case. However, what I am exposing here is what the Devil enjoyed doing.

He took our sin, this sin between me and this man, and then extended it to many more people in the body of believers at Forest Grove. It's a sad thing. And there are dozens of lies I could expose here that the Enemy propagated, but the lie that comes from my story in this time and this place is this lie that says you deserve condemnation, condemnation that moves past the beautiful sacrifice and atonement made for you by Jesus on the cross. Often when we receive that sort of condemnation, especially from fellow Christians, it looks like appropriate judgment of our sin, and we take that condemnation as if we are also receiving the judgment of the sin. Unfortunately, far too many believers make the same mistakes in passing out condemnation instead of judgment. When the offender, in this case me, believes this particular lie from the Enemy, then we forget Romans 8:1, that there is no condemnation for those who are in Christ. Instead we hear things more in line with, "Your sin was too great. You have to do something to atone for your sin." That's the lie.

"AND THE BUS KEPT GOING"

The human and fallen nature in me screamed that this little piece of paper was unfair, and part of me wanted Jeff to defend me, to ask the questions I simply couldn't ask, but he didn't. He just asked if we would be allowed to go back to our Sunday school class, which met right before the church service in an adjacent building, and Greg said that of course we could.

However, I was about to be crushed under the weight of all I had been asked to bear in the preceding three months. Jeff and the wife of the man with whom I'd had the affair (who, consequently, I had also been friends with, making my sin all the more grievous) were the victims, and rightly so. Jeff received calls and cards and visits, all telling him he was a saint for letting me stay. That had been hard to watch. After all, our marriage hadn't been a rose garden for a long, long time, and no marriage becomes that bad because of only one person. However, I was the one who committed the sin. I was the one who had made everything a public scandal that people saw. Knowing that, though, didn't make it any easier for me to sit back and watch.

Probably the hardest thing for me, though, was the reaction of the man with whom I had been having the affair once it came out. We've never spoken since that day, but the combination of his version of what happened and my silence made for some heart-wrenching months in my life.

But I deserved it, right? After all, I didn't know what was in his past, but I certainly knew what was in mine. This wasn't my only transgression. I had a long, long list of sins, and if my penance included taking my place on the pavement while the bus ran me over again and again and again, then I would lie down peacefully and take it.

But this? This seemed like too much. I felt like a criminal. I felt so much like the adulterous woman in John 8 who was thrown at the feet of Jesus by the angry crowd that demanded justice for her crime. No mention is made in this passage of Scripture about the man she was with. In those first eleven verses of John 8, the Bible says that the accusers caught her in the act and dragged her into the synagogue, throwing her at the feet of Jesus, who was teaching there. "Caught in the act" means an act was occurring, and that particular act requires two people, but she was the only one dragged into the temple. No partner was ever mentioned.

71

You see, I had learned from the story of the adulterous woman and had arrived at a beautiful truth, but I had landed on only the first part of that truth. The first part of the story caused me to believe the Enemy when he said I deserved every single condemnation and punishment that mankind could dole out—because like her, I had been caught in the act. Once the wife of the man I had been with found the letter he had written to me, the cat was out of the proverbial bag, and my partner and I had been caught. There was no more denying it.

Part of me wanted to pay for my crimes. That's the part Satan likes to capitalize on—our need to have some part in our redemption, some thing we can do so that we pay the penance due for the crimes we have committed. I was still trying to be in control. I was still trying to have some part in my own salvation, and the Devil loves to use that part of us against us. Paying for my crimes seemed right because I had sinned grievously and because part of the lie the Enemy told me was true.

I did deserve everything I was getting. But per his MO, Satan leaves out the rest of that truth, the truth that my Savior paid every debt I owe when He gave His precious life on the cross of Calvary. The more I heard, "You deserve this," the more I was determined to pay what I owed.

In retrospect, if I were to pan back and view the scene from a larger vantage point, it's clear that I was not the only one caught in this ugly snare. The high profile nature of my offense compelled everyone I had deceived to "weigh in" on the crime. Not surprisingly, the enemy cleverly assembled a cast of well-intentioned onlookers to scrutinize, refute, and even demonize my confession. Anyone remotely close to the situation was swept up in the scandalous aftermath. As conclusions were drawn, so were spoken and unspoken lines of loyalty. Satan was having a field day! The lies were piling up, one right on top of the other.

"NEITHER DO I CONDEMN YOU"

Let me return to the story of the adulterous woman in John 8. In verses two and three, John relates that the Pharisees had caught this woman in the act of adultery and then dragged her, most likely naked, into the midst of the synagogue and placed her at the feet of Jesus. John records their words in verses four through five,

"Teacher, this woman has been caught in the act of adultery. Now in the Law, Moses commanded us to stone such women. So what do you say?"

Jesus seemed to disregard them for a few minutes, bending over and writing something in the dirt with his finger. They wouldn't be ignored, however, so they kept insisting that he give them an answer. Finally, in verse seven, he answered,

"Let him who is without sin among you be the first to throw a stone at her."

Since Jesus was speaking to the sin of judgment that we are all guilty of at one time or another, these Pharisees correctly dropped their stones and left. This is a beautiful message, and it's certainly one we should all remember. However, there is so much more to this story. The second part of the story, when understood in its entirety, can set all of us free from this lie that binds—the lie that says that we deserve condemnation because of who we are, so we had better buck up and take our condemnation.

Once all of the Pharisees had dropped their murderous stones and walked away, Jesus was left alone with this naked, adulterous woman. She was most likely beaten and bruised, and any sense of dignity and self-respect she may have had was gone. Unlike the Pharisees, Jesus stayed, bent over, and started writing in the dirt again with his finger.

At some point while he was writing, the woman stood up, most likely to slink away in embarrassment and guilt. Jesus, however, wasn't finished with her. I love that He wasn't. He's not finished with you or me either. He stopped writing, stood up, and asked her in verse ten,

"Woman, where are they? Has no one condemned you?"

I'm sure she looked around the empty synagogue at that point, maybe realizing for the first time that everyone had indeed left. She told him that no one was left, and then it was His next statement that is astounding. He simply says in verse eleven,

"Neither do I condemn you; go, and from now on sin no more."

How could He say such a thing? How could He look at her and say that her sin would not be held against her and that she wouldn't have to pay the penalty for that sin? This woman's guilt was real! My guilt was real! Your guilt is real! According to the Law of Moses, this woman deserved death. Jesus would have known this. He would have known the Scripture in Deuteronomy 22:22 that states,

If a man is found lying with the wife of another man, both of them shall die, the man who lay with the woman, and the woman. So you shall purge the evil from Israel.

How could Jesus possibly say that He did not condemn her, considering what was written in the Law? Here's where the news is really good—good for me and good for you. And believe me, Satan doesn't want us to know that good news. Satan is content with our stopping at the condemnation place, because then it's pretty easy to get us to pick up the gauntlet of paying

The lie is that we deserve condemnation, so instead of seeing who we are in Christ, we live in an identity stained by the sins we've committed.

for our sins in our own strength. The lie is that we deserve condemnation, so instead of seeing who we are in Christ, we live in an identity stained by the sins we've committed.

In the case of the woman in John 8, God fully intended for this sin of adultery to be punished to the full extent of the law, but she would not bear her punishment. She would not pay her penalty. Jesus, this young teacher, would be punished in her place because He loved her with an unparalleled love. He did so because He had already chosen her from before time began to be His, because He would be the one to pay the penalty for her sin, and because He *did* pay the penalty for her sin only a few short years later.

The truth is that in this woman's situation, as well as in my situation and yours, regardless of the hidden agendas of the people around us or the overt agenda of the Devil himself, the accused ones were and are guilty. Because of this woman's guilt, she deserved death. I was guilty of what I was accused of. Chances are, so are you. All of us deserve the punishment for our various sins, not only those punishments that are meted out on stupid pieces of paper, like the one telling me where to park and what service to attend, but also the punishment of death. My sins, all of them, deserve eternal separation from my Bridegroom.

However, here stood a man this woman in John 8 didn't even know and had done nothing for, yet this man forgave her. This man, this Jesus, fully intended to and did pay the debt she owed. The truth is that she was given cleanness in that instant. She became a new creature, justified in God's eyes. Wearing Jesus' righteousness, the Father viewed her as if she had never sinned, but also as if she had perfectly obeyed. All of this because Jesus became sin for her, perfectly obeying the Father on her behalf.

Why would Jesus forgive her and take her punishment upon Himself, and why does the Devil want us lost in half the truth, which is an entire lie? Jesus took our punishment on the cross. He did that for you and for me and for that woman outside of the Mount of Olives because His love is our identity. His love is who we are, not the sins we commit or those that have been committed against us.

I AM BECAUSE HE LOVES

Jeff and I did return to Forest Grove Church the very next Sunday, and I'm not going to lie to you: it was horrible. Walking through the parking lot to head into church that first time felt like walking a gang plank. When we got inside the church, I was jeered at, heckled, told to leave, and told that I had no business being there. One young woman even threw a bulletin at me. I sat through the church service, fighting the urge to run out of there as fast as my legs could carry me.

My Jeff never left me in those early days. I know it had to be so hard on him, standing beside a woman who had betrayed him in every way imaginable, enduring the pain of staying when he must have wanted to bolt. But he did stay. He stayed, he says now, because God told him to and he obeyed. I stayed because I was at the end of my rope and God told me to. I obeyed.

We returned to Forest Grove Church not because we wanted to, but because God told us to and we obeyed. However, my truth also comes from a little bit of introspection. I was still listening to that insidious lie from

Satan that told me to stay at Forest Grove for all the wrong reasons. We stayed for two long years before God released us to go elsewhere, and I learned much of what I now know about leaning on the Love that never leaves me and never forsakes me. God orchestrated and used that time, to be sure, but I didn't stay on some moral high ground that I was trying to get closer to God, though that was definitely what was happening. No, I stayed because I wanted to allow what I saw as the "payment" I thought I owed for my crimes. Every insult, every look or word or document of condemnation became an instrument by which I could pay what I thought I owed for my sins.

I walked into the loving arms of a Savior who didn't have to catch me because He had never let me go in the first place.

The lie told me that I had to pay, and that my payment came in condemnation and works within that condemnation. The beautiful truth that Satan didn't want me to know was that my payment had already been fulfilled in Christ. I should have stayed for reconciliation and to allow peace, and at some level, I think I was. However, mostly I stayed because I wanted to pay what I thought I owed. I stayed because I listened to that small, malicious whisper from Satan that said, "You deserve this. Be quiet and take it."

In some sense, I did walk the plank that Sunday morning, but I didn't walk into treacherous waters leading to death. I walked into the loving arms of a Savior who didn't have to catch me because He had never let me go in the first place.

I was counseling a young woman not long ago who had a similar background to mine. She had been caught in the act and had been basically shunned by her church family as a result. It turned out that her father was the pastor of the church she had belonged to, and even though he endured a lot of pain and heartache and was almost relieved of his position as senior pastor because of her transgressions, he stood by her through it all. Regardless of her father's love, she still left the church, and when she and I met, she had been wandering from church to church, trying unsuccessfully to find a home.

Her past was well in the past, and in talking to her, I could tell that what she really wanted was to return to her home church. Her family was still there, and her father was still the pastor. She was scared though. She was worried about how she would be treated and what it would be like. I told her my story, and then I told her that I felt she should return. There truly is a myriad of reasons for one to do so, but it's easy to think of lots of reasons not to as well. But what I saw in front of me was a beautiful young lady who through her experiences had found the love of a Savior who did not condemn her based on past mistakes. That, I said, was what the members of that church needed to see. Most of the people who condemned her and her father for standing by her had long since left, so that wasn't really going to be an issue. However, many of the original families still attended. I finally convinced her that the impact of seeing her now, as a well-adjusted, forgiven bride of Christ, would be a wonderful testimony to the power of that kind of love.

I convinced her to return and to hold her head high—not in defiance, but in peace. She should be able to walk in to any place, even if it was filled with people who wanted her head on a stake, and portray what a person who is truly redeemed can portray. She could do that. I could do that. And both of us should do that, because if our mistakes and our subsequent deliverance do not serve to advance the love of the only One who can set us free from both guilt and condemnation, then our mistakes count for nothing. This beautiful young lady did return, and I had the pleasure of being there the morning she did. I couldn't have been prouder, and I know that our Savior smiled when she took that step of faith.

Understand that there are repercussions for our actions. There will always be consequences for the sins we commit, and unfortunately, we are often called upon to bear the consequences of the sins that others commit against us. We live in a fallen and imperfect world, and cause and effect remain in play. However, don't believe the lie that you deserve condemnation and that you must receive it—not if you have first believed on the Savior who went to the cross on your behalf.

Each and every time we put on a stiff upper lip and take the berating and yelling and pain inflicted on us by others because of our sins, it is the same as looking our wonderful Savior in the face and saying, "Thanks a bunch for dying on the cross to bear the penalty for my sins. It was a beautiful gesture, but I've got this. I'll take the condemnation instead."

Let the Lord be your vindicator and allow the wagging tongues to wag, but in your heart, rest in the knowledge of the moment you accepted the loving sacrifice of Jesus Christ. Your Savior is the One who paid the penalty you rightfully ought to pay, but at that moment you were justified in the sight of the only One who matters, the God of the universe and the Maker of heaven and earth.

Don't let a confused and frustrated world identify who you are, even if that confused and frustrated world consists of confused and frustrated Christians. Your identity is in Jesus. He is your Savior and the Lover of your soul. He took your punishment so that you would spend eternity loving Him and being loved by Him. That is truth, and that is the truth that will break the bonds that the Enemy's lies have placed on you. Break them now and meditate instead on what is true—once and for all.

GETTING
FREE

There is deliverance for all who will seek it. Won't you seek deliverance now from the lie that brings condemnation on God's children by praying the prayer to the right? God is right there, right now, lovingly offering you freedom from this lie that has bound you for far too long. Offer this prayer to your Father and embrace the freedom that is yours. Then allow His Word to spring forth more truth in your heart as you meditate on His love from Scripture in the verses that follow.

My Father,

What an amazing Lover of my soul you are! You are gracious and filled with loving kindness toward those who are Yours and who follow in Your commandments. You have forgiven my sins once and for all as Jesus, Your Son and my Savior, sacrificed Himself on the Cross of Calvary so that I might live. I know that the moment I accepted this incredible truth, I became justified in Your sight. You view me now not only as if I'd never sinned but also as if I'd always obeyed. Thank You, my Jesus, my Lord, for this eternal gift. I renounce the lie right now that the Enemy has been telling me—that I must pay the penalty for these sins. I break the bonds that have held me in condemnation, in the Name of Jesus, and instead I replace those chains with the knowledge of truth, the truth that there is no condemnation for those who are in Christ Jesus. This is life-giving truth, and it is freeing truth, and these are the things that will guide me and characterize my life from this moment forward.

I declare these things in the precious name of Jesus Christ, my Propitiator and the Lover of my soul.
Amen.

SCRIPTURES FOR MEDITATION

*If we confess our sins, he is faithful and
just to forgive us our sins and to cleanse us
from all unrighteousness.*
– 1 John 1:9

*But God, being rich in mercy, because of
the great love with which he loved us, even
when we were dead in our trespasses, made
us alive together with Christ—by grace you
have been saved—and raised us up with
him and seated us with him in the heavenly
places in Christ Jesus, so that in the coming
ages he might show the immeasurable riches
of his grace in kindness toward us in Christ
Jesus. For by grace you have been saved
through faith. And this is not your own
doing; it is the gift of God, not a result of
works, so that no one may boast.*
– Ephesians 2:4-9

For God so loved the world, that he gave his only Son, that whoever believes in him should not perish but have eternal life. For God did not send his Son into the world to condemn the world, but in order that the world might be saved through him. Whoever believes in him is not condemned, but whoever does not believe is condemned already, because he has not believed in the name of the only Son of God.

– John 3:16-18

There is therefore now no condemnation for those who are in Christ Jesus. For the law of the Spirit of life has set you free in Christ Jesus from the law of sin and death. For God has done what the law, weakened by the flesh, could not do. By sending his own Son in the likeness of sinful flesh and for sin, he condemned sin in the flesh, in order that the righteous requirement of the law might be fulfilled in us, who walk not according to the flesh but according to the Spirit.

– Romans 8:1-4

CHAPTER FIVE

LIE #5

"It's Too Late"

"What Do I Do With This?"

The price of a prostitute is only a loaf of bread, but a married woman hunts down a precious life. –Proverbs 6:26

To keep you from the forbidden woman, from the adulteress with her smooth words. –Proverbs 7:5

For the lips of a forbidden woman drip honey, and her speech is smoother than oil, but in the end she is bitter as wormwood, sharp as a two-edged sword. –Proverbs 5:3-4

If a man commits adultery with the wife of his neighbor, both the adulterer and the adulteress shall surely be put to death. –Leviticus 20:10

Let marriage be held in honor among all, and let the marriage bed be undefiled, for God will judge the sexually immoral and the adulterous.
–Hebrews 13:4

Then I will draw near to you for judgment. I will be a swift witness against the sorcerers, against the adulterers, against those who swear falsely...
–Malachi 3:5

And on and on it went. Verse after verse. Page after page. I couldn't stop reading, mostly because I kept waiting on the redemption part. But it never came. This email went on for what equaled seven full pages of Scripture upon Scripture condemning the adulterer to death.

It had been about six months since my last affair had been uncovered: six months of painstaking work and effort in my marriage, six months of despair and depression over the abandonment I felt from the man who left me to take all of the blame, six months of slow, but steady healing, and then I received this email.

A new school year had begun by this point, and I had gone to part-time so that I could work on my Master's degree. On a Thursday afternoon around 4:00, I was sitting at my computer doing homework. Jeff was already home from work. He was downstairs in the garage working on something. He stayed there a lot for those first months. We had truly come a long way, though certainly we still had a long, long way to go in our marriage. Still, things were better than they had been.

We had been back to church for about three months, and while the transition was pretty awful, the sensational nature of the scandal seemed to finally be dying down. I was the big talk for a while, and I received a lot of unwanted attention, but one thing about humans is, we have a very short attention span. Eventually something else happened to turn the gossip mill away from me, so people were starting to return to the more comfortable treatment of ignoring me instead of slinging insults at me every time I went to church.

My one lone friend who had stood by me at the first had steadily been joined by a few more. Eventually people began to realize that I wasn't a devil-worshipping harlot who was after all of their husbands. That was good. My children were starting to get over the uncertainty of whether or not Mommy was sticking around. I wish they had been immune to the insults and slander that was thrown in my direction, but they were not. It was traumatic for them for a while, but things were starting to look a little normal, or at least as normal as they could at this stage of the game.

When I took a break from the assignment I was working on, I decided to open my email. I saw an email from an address I didn't recognize, a Yahoo account with no name attached to it. This took place a while ago, before we were afraid to open an unknown email for fear of a virus being launched on every electronic device we owned, so I opened it. I was curious. The subject line simply said, "Adultery."

Now it might seem weird that I would even open something with that subject line, but remember, I was still of the mindset that I deserved the wrath of every Tom, Dick, and Harry out there. Even though they were fewer in number, I was still taking whatever calls and letters I received demanding retribution for my crimes. Most of the people who contacted me weren't malicious. As ill-mannered as their attempts were, their intentions were generally honorable. Almost all of them wanted either to help me come to repentance or to be assured that I had gotten there. With that in mind, I opened the email.

What I saw was a list of Bible verses similar to those at the beginning of this chapter, but much, much more comprehensive. What I came to realize as I read these passages of Scripture was that this was a methodical re-cap of every passage in the Bible condemning the adulterer to hell. Eventually I stopped reading every word and started skimming. I wanted to get past all of these verses of condemnation and get to the good part, the ones about repentance and forgiveness. In my mind, the motivation behind sending someone like me an email like that had to be in thinking that I hadn't yet repented and needed to be made aware of what that would entail. Of course, I had repented, but I just figured the writer didn't know that.

However, I got to the end of the list of condemning verses, and they stopped abruptly. The last one was from Revelation 2:22,

Behold, I will throw her onto a sickbed, and those who commit adultery with her I will throw into great tribulation, unless they repent of her works.

And that was that. The email just ended. I scrolled down a little more, absolutely positive that the redemptive passages would be there. Otherwise, what was the point of this email? But there were no redemptive passages. The verse from Revelation was the last thing on the email.

I sat back in my chair and just stared at the screen. I looked again at the address for the sender but quickly realized it was from an anonymous email account. There would be no way for me to trace where it had come from. Please understand where I was at this point. I was entrenching myself in God and His Word. I had finally and completely gotten to the end of my rope, and when all those plates came crashing down to the ground, I was determined not to pick them up again. Instead, I was trying as best as I could to start afresh.

At forty years old, I thought I had wasted pretty much my entire life trying to find happiness, and part of me had given in to the idea that happiness wasn't ever going to be in the cards for me. The best I could hope for was to try to make up for the pain I had caused my remaining friends and family and to move forward. The point is, I was leaning totally on anything and everything God said to guide and guard me in those days, just as we should each and every day. I was desperate, however. I was hanging onto the Word like the life preserver it is, and I was not about to let go this time. Consequently, what struck me from the very moment I read that email was that I was strictly reading God's Word. No commentary was added. It was just a list of verse after verse that pertained to adultery and what judgment would be levied against those engaged in it.

After all, the Devil is crafty, so he had a few more lies he was going to try to slip by me in those days. This lie was cloaked in the very Words of God, which is something the Devil has done before. He was an angel, and the Bible says that the demons know God's Word better than we do. You can bet Satan knows it even better than that. He even tried to use God's Word against God Himself when the temptation of Jesus took place in the wilderness just before His ministry here on earth began.

How arrogant the Devil is! How conceited he must be to think that he could use the very Words of our Lord to trick Jesus. Of course, that didn't work, but I'm not Jesus, so I'm not nearly as smart or as quick to see what was going on. Instead, I panicked. This was God's Word I was reading, and I didn't have to read much between the lines to see what was in store for people who did what I had done. Judgment—plain and simple. Hell. End of story.

I couldn't help myself. I read the email again. Then I read it again and again and again. I kept thinking that surely I had missed something in those verses that said there was a way out of this mess. Surely there was something in there about repentance and forgiveness, even for the adulteress. But there wasn't. It seemed from what I was reading that I had stumbled on the one sin for which God had no time, the one sin for which He had no pardon, and I was condemned.

I kept saying over and over again, "What do I do with this? What am I supposed to do with this? This is God's Word! Where am I to go after this?" I could feel the anxiety building. I could feel my heart palpitating, my breathing becoming more and more labored. I was truly panicking, and I didn't know what to do next.

Finally, I decided I should call someone. My friend, the one who had called me the day after the affair went public, the woman who had become my mentor and my rock in the middle of this horror show—she was the one I decided to call. She, too, was a teacher, and I knew she most likely was still at school, but class was over, so I hoped she would pick up her phone. It rang and rang, but there was no answer. There was one other woman I could risk calling, but she didn't answer either. Jeff. I would go downstairs and talk to Jeff. We weren't bosom buddies at this time, but we were doing Bible study together, and he was a good, solid Christian man. I felt certain that at least he could shed some light on what I was supposed to do with this list of verses.

To my great disappointment, I came down to find that the garage was empty, and Jeff's truck was gone. Later I would find out that he had run to Home Depot to pick something up, but the only thing I saw was that he was gone. I had no one to talk to, no one to bring me to reason.

I ran back upstairs, and there were the verses, still staring back at me from the computer screen. I sat down at my vanity a few feet from my desk and put my head in my hands. "God!" I screamed. "God, why would You let someone send me that? Why would You want me to read that? What am I supposed to do with that? It's Your Word!"

FREEDOM AND ANNE BANCROFT

I started sobbing uncontrollably at that point. There didn't seem to be anywhere I could go to get away from this message. I couldn't reason my way out of it. I couldn't even think straight, and no one was answering their phone to help me figure out what to do with it. I cried and cried, and I kept occasionally yelling, "Why?" toward the ceiling, but the pain wouldn't abate. Then the most awful words I'd ever imagined became my reality: It's too late. I have done the unimaginable, and now, it is quite simply too late.

At that very moment, my head was filled with an image. I recognized the face in the image immediately as Mary Magdalene, and the way I knew it was Mary Magdalene was because the face actually belonged to Anne Bancroft. I had seen an old movie years earlier, depicting the life of Jesus. In this movie, called *Jesus*, Anne Bancroft played Mary Magdalene. The image that filled my head was Anne Bancroft dressed as Mary Magdalene from that movie. I stopped crying and sat up. Just as quickly as the image filled my head, a voice was there, too. This wonderful voice simply said, *Debbie, I loved this woman. She was a sinner, shunned by society, but I loved her with a love unparalleled. I loved her like I love you. Your sin was what you did. In me, you have become what you are, and I love you.*

Just as soon as the voice finished speaking, my phone started ringing. I didn't answer it at first. I was too mesmerized by what had just happened. My tears continued, but they were now tears of joy. I was filled at that moment with the love God had shown me that night months before when I had cried out to him. That night He had given me a glimpse of His love in a dream, but this time He spoke to me when I was awake, and I knew. I knew and felt and experienced the love of my Savior, and for the first time in my life, I really knew who I was, who I am.

Eventually I realized that the phone was ringing. I don't know how long it had been ringing, but when I finally answered, my mentor was on the other end.

"Debbie!" she yelled, "Are you okay? I had a clear feeling that you weren't okay, and then I saw that I missed a call!"

"I'm fine, at least I'm fine now." I then told her from beginning to end what had transpired over the course of the last few minutes. Her first instinct was to lead me in prayer for the person who had sent that email. I hadn't thought about doing that, but as usual, this friend went to wisdom first and emotion later.

After we prayed, she and I talked about the verses, about the image of Mary Magdalene, and about the beautiful privilege of having our Father speak to us and assure us of His love in such tangible ways. She was right, of course. It was a divine privilege and one I thank Him for still every day.

WHEN IT'S "IN THE BOOKS"

But as I was studying for this book and asking God exactly which lies I was to expose, this one was to be the last because this one proves to be the most devastating. When we look at our lives and the things we have done, we are looking at things in the past. We are examining things we have done, as in we can't take them back. They're in the books. That can be a dangerous place to be, and it's a ripe and plentiful playground for the Devil and his lies.

Have you ever said something and wished the minute you said it that you could take it back? The words are out there floating around, and the only thing you wish is that you could fabricate some ethereal butterfly net and bring them right back into your great big mouth? Maybe a better example today is when you are texting someone and you accidentally hit "Send" before you're ready? It's gone. It's out there. Barring the recipient's magically dropping her phone in the toilet or in a swimming pool or on the road where it gets run over by a tractor-trailer truck, you are now toast.

Those may be very flippant examples, but our sins can be like that. We can become convinced that we've finally gone too far and it's too late.

How many times are people expected to forgive you? How many times can you betray and lie to those you love and still have them welcome you back into their lives? When is the next drink the one that's too far? When is the last pill the one that pushes you over the edge? When is it just too late when it comes to God?

When is it just too late when it comes to God?

Whereas we definitely can walk over an edge into the "too late" zone when it comes to people, the wonderful news is that there is no such line that can be crossed with our Savior. Romans 5:8 reminds us,

But God shows his love for us in that while we were still sinners, Christ died for us.

Did you catch that? While we were still sinners. That means that while we were still in the midst of sinning—when Jesus already knew that you and I were going to have sins "in the books"—He still willingly went to the cross so that we might live. Friends, Jesus also said that He didn't come for the righteous but for the unrighteous. He came because we need Him, and there's no such thing as too far gone.

I like to say that we are never knocked off the game board where Jesus is concerned. Sure, we may have to go back to "Start," but we're still playing! He never takes our game piece off the game board, folds the game board up, and goes home because we are so bad at the rules. When we sin we simply start over. We start over, but God never fails or stops loving us. He loves us as much as the guy who never seems to have to go back to the beginning when he plays.

And when it comes to those Jesus chooses to use in His kingdom-building work, we need go no further than the apostles to see that He prefers those of us who are a little rough around the edges. When Jesus was teaching by the Lake of Gennesaret, He didn't look out into the crowd, which was more than likely filled with teachers of the law and high ranking officials in the synagogue, and call any of them to follow Him. Nope. He looked out over the crowds and chose some fishermen!

I'm not sure how many of you have been around men who fish for a living, but they tend to be a little "salty," if you'll pardon the pun. Just look at that popular television show, "Deadliest Catch." If you've ever watched that show, then you have seen a pretty good picture of the types of men and women who fish as their chosen profession. They tend to be a little on the rough side, and Jesus walked right through that crowd of people and directly approached Peter and his fishermen buddies.

One of the things I noticed in the account in Luke 5 is that Jesus was teaching by the lake, but Peter and his buddies weren't necessarily paying attention to Him. I'm sure they knew who this Teacher was since He had already been teaching for a while, but Luke 5:2 says,

And he [Jesus] saw two boats by the lake, but the fishermen had gone out of them and were washing their nets.

In other words, these fishermen were going about their trade while Jesus was teaching. However, Jesus wasn't interested in those who didn't think they needed Him. He was interested in those who didn't yet have a testimony they could share. He wanted those who had a story on which He could put the finishing touches. He was and still is interested in those of us who need Him and lean on Him and can tell our stories to others so that they will know of Him.

BUILDING YOUR STORY

When I traveled to Africa a few months ago, I taught a series of messages there called "Building Your Story." The emphasis was on looking at our lives not as a mess or as a compilation of our tragedy and sin, but as stories that God is building so that He can use them. The Apostles were men with stories God was building. Abraham was like that. David was like that. The woman at the well was like that. Job was like that.

We can't always see what God is doing in our lives today, but we can be assured that not one thing in the lives of His children is wasted.

We can't always see what God is doing in our lives today, but we can be assured that not one thing in the lives of His children is wasted. That includes your sin. For those of us who love God and are called according to His purpose, He will work all things out for good. (Romans 8:28) Every single thing that has happened in your life, whether that something is something you did or something that was done to you, it is a part of your story, a story that is unique to you and can only be used by you. In such a beautiful way, God can use the many components of your story to speak to men and women everywhere about this wonderful and awesome Savior who walked right through the throngs of more likely candidates and chose you. He chose me too, and I am now in the throes of allowing Him to use me and the components of my story.

If I would have believed the Enemy that day when he told me it was too late, I would have given up, and I would never have gotten the chance to share my testimony with thousands of women all over the world. God made that possible. Jesus made that possible, but He did it because I refused to believe the lies that Satan was trying to get me to buy into. Don't you believe them either.

No matter where you are right now in your Christian life, no matter what you did last year or last month or last week or yesterday or last night or two minutes ago, it is not too late. Throw down the gauntlet. Do battle right now with Satan—right this very instant—and break this final chain. Jesus loves the ones the Enemy tries to throw away. Jesus died for you, loves you, chose you, and will use your story to help someone, but only if you allow Him to do so. Pray this prayer now, denouncing this lie, and think on the truth of who it is that walked through the crowds to get to you. God bless you and your story.

GETTING
FREE

Pray the prayer to the right now, denouncing the lie that it is too late, and think on the truth of who it is that walked through the crowds to get to _you_. Our Father has a plan for you, even you, in all that has happened to you and all that you have gone through. Your life is _your story_, and God is pleased to use you. God bless you and your story.

My Father,

What a loving and gracious Father You are! You are mighty and beyond description in Your attributes of kindness and forbearance. Thank You for walking through a crowd of people who I might think are so much more worthy than I and choosing me as Your bride. Jesus, You are my everlasting to everlasting, and I thank You for building my story. I thank You for the truth that I am never too late or too bad or too far gone for Your love and forgiveness. I do ask You now to forgive me of my shortcomings and for every way I deny Your power in my life today. Help me see the ways in which I deny You and give me the wisdom and discernment to identify and change them. Right now I denounce the lies of the Enemy that say I have sinned too much to be Your bride. I break that bond at this moment, in the great and mighty name of Jesus Christ, and instead I fasten the belt of truth to my waist. I declare boldly that I see Your love and Your acceptance, and I acknowledge that You have given those to me. Thank You for building my story. Give me opportunities to help someone else see the lies that are binding them and help me show them how they can be introduced to freedom. Thank You, Jesus. I love You, and I declare all of this as my banner, just as Your banner over me is love.

In Jesus Christ's Name, I pray, Amen.

SCRIPTURES FOR MEDITATION

He brought me to the banqueting house,
and his banner over me was love.
— Song of Solomon 2:4

But if we walk in the light, as he is in the light, we
have fellowship with one another, and the blood
of Jesus his Son cleanses us from all sin.
— 1 John 1:7

My little children, I am writing these things to
you so that you may not sin. But if anyone does
sin, we have an advocate with the Father,
Jesus Christ the righteous.
— 1 John 2:1

For all have sinned and fall short of the glory
of God, and are justified by his grace as a gift,
through the redemption that is in Christ Jesus,
whom God put forward as a propitiation by
his blood, to be received by faith. This was to
show God's righteousness, because in his divine
forbearance he had passed over former sins. It
was to show his righteousness at the present time,
so that he might be just and the justifier of the one
who has faith in Jesus.
— Romans 3:23-26

This is the covenant that I will make with them after those days, declares the Lord: I will put my laws on their hearts, and write them on their minds, then he adds, I will remember their sins and their lawless deeds no more.
– Hebrews 10:16-17

For I know the plans I have for you, declares the LORD, plans for welfare and not for evil, to give you a future and a hope. Then you will call upon me and come and pray to me, and I will hear you. You will seek me and find me, when you seek me with all your heart. I will be found by you, declares the LORD.
– Jeremiah 29:11-14a

But when he [Jesus] heard it, he said, "Those who are well have no need of a physician, but those who are sick. Go and learn what this means: 'I desire mercy, and not sacrifice.' For I came not to call the righteous, but sinners."
– Matthew 9:12-13

For because he [Jesus] himself has suffered when tempted, he is able to help those who are being tempted.
– Hebrews 2:18

CHAPTER SIX

The Truth that Sets You FREE

You are Valuable.

Just like every one of us, there came a first time in my life where my innocence was taken from me. Because we live in a fallen world alongside of fallen creatures, we all have many opportunities either to have our dreams shattered or to be the one who shatters someone else's dreams. When those things occur, the lie of worthlessness gains another brick until finally it is nothing less than a monstrosity.

What I propose to you right now is that the very things that the Enemy chooses to use to lie to us about our value are actually the things that prove our extreme and necessary worth. After all, we know from the story of Joseph in Genesis 50 that what man or the Devil means for evil, God intends for good. (Genesis 50:20). My proposal then is that those things in your life that are made to look like they devalue you are actually intended by God because you are, in fact, so *very valuable to Him.*

Let's take Job for instance. As this story begins, we are introduced to a man named Job who is very wealthy. He had many children, a wife, lots of cattle and sheep and land, and he knew the Lord. He walked steadfastly in the ways of the Lord. As the story continues, we are transported to a heavenly scene, and in this scene, all of the angels are coming before the Lord, presenting themselves to Him. Satan had not been cast out yet, so he was one of those angels coming before God. We can already see the character of this angel, however—a character that will lead to his final fall.

But in the story at hand, God addresses Satan, asking him where he was coming from, to which Satan replied that he had been traveling around the earth, looking at all of the created things. Once God heard that Satan had been down on the earth, God's first thought was of Job. His immediate response was,

Have you considered my servant Job, that there is none like him on the earth, a blameless and upright man, who fears God and turns away from evil? (Job 1:8)

Satan argued that of course Job was a great guy. God had blessed him! The angel then proposed that God take away all of those blessings so they would see if Job was truly as devoted to God as God thought.

As the Bible tells us, God gave Satan permission to torment Job terribly. He was allowed to take Job's children, his livestock, his money, his houses, and even his health. The only thing he wasn't allowed to take was Job's life.

It's a difficult thing to read the book of Job. That man suffered horribly, and he never knew why. In the middle of all that was taken from him, he never cursed God, but he certainly spent a lot of time crying out to God and asking why. *Why are these things happening?* He begged God to take his life—or better yet, to make it so that Job had never been born. His friends turned against him, his wife turned against him, and eventually the entire village turned their backs on him.

What I want to call to your attention was the part of this story that Job never knew. He was never privy to the heavenly conversation that took place. He didn't know that the reason these things were happening to him wasn't because he was being punished or cast out in some way. God was allowing these things to happen because *He trusted Job*. God trusted His servant Job so much that He allowed tragedy after tragedy to happen to him. God knew that He would be able to use Job and his story someday. And do you see what happened? Millions of people have read the story of Job; his testimony of constancy and his trust in God's sovereign power despite tremendous adversity have become the mainstay for any study on persevering in faith through the trials in this life.

I believe that one of the reasons God has included the book of Job in His complete Holy Word is so that you and I might have access to the heavenly conversation that happened prior to the tragedies that hit Job's life. Job didn't know about that conversation. Likewise, you and I have no idea what is actually happening in heaven when our lives become horrible. And please hear me, it does not matter whether or not your life is horrible because of something you did or because of something that was done against you. A horrible life is a horrible life, but for the Christian, there is always a heavenly conversation.

What I know now is that it hurt God when those boys molested me that morning in 1974, but I also believe there was a conversation that was going on that I couldn't hear.

Do you see my Deb? I love my Deb. I created her strong and tenacious, and because I trust her so much, I will allow many tragedies to fall on her, and I will do so because she is valuable to Me. I will use her to My glory, and her life will be the balm that soothes many hearts. Do you see My Deb? I love My Deb. I will use My Deb.

It is difficult to write those words without crying because they bring me such joy. They are also in direct contradiction to what the Devil wanted me to believe in the midst of every sin I've committed and every sin committed against me. Satan wanted me to believe that I was worthless and without value. But what I know now is that God has been building my story, just as He is building your story, because He trusts me to do His work while here on earth. The great happiness that brings me when I think of it far overshadows the pain and misery of past years.

This is called having a "heavenly perspective" or an "eternal perspective," and this perspective is our biggest and best tool against the lies of the Enemy. I know that this perspective on my life is true because I believe the Bible is true. Romans 8:28 is in every Bible, in every translation. We either believe that "for those who love God all things work together for good, for those who are called according to his purpose," or we don't. We either believe what God declares in Jeremiah 29:11—that He has plans for us and that those plans are to give us a hope and a future and not to harm us—or we don't. You can't have it both ways. Believe me, if you want to get out from under the influence of the Enemy's lie that says you are worthless, then believe the truth from our Father that you are valuable and most especially that you are valuable to Him.

YOU ARE A REFLECTION OF CHRIST

It takes a lot of effort to come to the realization that as a believer in Christ, your image and your identity are not the sum of all of your experiences. Your image and your identity are Jesus. But as we discussed in chapter two, the world tells us that image is everything because what others think of us is extremely important. The lie the Enemy convinces many of us with is that we have to create and maintain a variety of images, depending on the people we are with.

However, I want to take that a step further. I contend that even as Christians, we have been convinced that an image of Christ just isn't enough. We live as if being like Christ and showing the world the humility of Christ and the love of Christ isn't sufficient. We contend that His image won't supply us with popularity or money or success. After all, those are the world's dreams, and if we want something more than simple Christian things, then we may have to bend the rules a little so that we can have money or things or popularity.

Even further than that, I think that many of us also believe that our past precludes any notion that we can portray a Christ-like image to the world, at least not one of any authenticity and usefulness. *Only the "good Christians" can be missionaries or pastors or leaders or teachers. I'll just be over here serving coffee or stacking chairs. I've done some pretty terrible stuff in my past, so that disqualifies me from the "big" service in church.* That's a lie, and one of Satan's favorites! All of these misconceptions are bound up in the lie of image, and I want to tell you the truth about who you are in Christ and how amazing His reflection is in your life *right now!*

Do you remember the story of the woman at the well in John 4? Jesus waited alone at a well in Samaria while the disciples went off into town to find something to eat. Jesus met a woman at the well, and He knew immediately that she was a woman who was trying to avoid the eyes of others. She was drawing water around noon, during the heat of the day, and that was not ordinarily when the other women would be there.

So Jesus struck up a conversation with her, and within this conversation, He revealed to her that He knew about her past: she had five husbands over the course of her life, and the one she was living with now wasn't her husband. Eventually, Jesus offered her living water, which is salvation in Him. As a matter of fact, when Jesus told her in John 4:26 that He was the Messiah, this was the first time recorded in the Bible that He had revealed that to anyone. He chose this woman that no one else would even talk to—a Samaritan living in sexual sin—and revealed to her who He was. And she believed.

But what can we learn about her image and who she really was? She ran into town after meeting Jesus and accepting the gift of living water He had offered her, and she proceeded to tell everyone she saw about this Jesus. She went everywhere yelling, "Come see a man who told me all that I ever did. Can this be the Christ?" (John 4:29)

The townspeople knew who this woman was. They knew she had been sleeping around and that she was of questionable moral character, but look what happens when this woman who now knows Jesus tells them about Him. In John 4:39 we read,

Many Samaritans from that town believed in him because of the woman's testimony.

Many *Samaritans*, a race of people who quite frankly couldn't stand the Jews any more than the Jews could stand them, believed in Him. And they came to believe on Jesus because of this woman's testimony. Because of her story. Because God had been building her story and she now reflected Christ, the past didn't matter except to magnify the grace, mercy, and love of the Savior.

When this woman ran throughout the town proclaiming the good news of Jesus Christ as Messiah, her image was no longer tied to her past, even though her past was still her past. Her image now reflected the One who had saved her, and that was what people responded to. That's what she displayed to the people in the village, and that's what caused them to return to talk to Him and eventually believe on Him.

Unfortunately, so many of us go through life creating different personae that will bring us attention or serve to make us loved, and then we go through that same life begrudgingly maintaining those different images. The truth is that our image is not defined by what we have done or what has been done to us, but our image is defined by what was done *for* us. If we can but see and understand that the love that saved us is the love that shows on our face and in our life, then maybe we might move beyond our own pain.

I am often lauded and congratulated these days for my transparency about my past when, truthfully, it's not the transparency that's so wonderful. It's the change in focus that is so wonderful. My transparency has come because my past no longer defines me. Jesus defines me, and because I have finally allowed Him to be the One whom I display, telling about parts of the story that might be useful to others is somewhat of a breeze.

You see, it *is* all about image, but it's all about the image of Jesus that we show to others *because of our past*, not in spite of our past. If you know Jesus as your Savior, then the image of His love and mercy is all over your face every single day. Realize that your past also belongs to Him and that it can be used to let others see Him.

He is who you are! What a glorious and freeing truth! It is this truth that combats the lie about worldly images. Instead, shine forth in the glory of who you are and Whose face you reflect by way of your story and your love for Him. It's not about transparency. It's about reflection, and your reflection is Jesus.

YOU ARE NOT ALONE

One truth that is as sure as the day is long in summer is that a person will be lonely when he or she buys the lie about being strong. We build walls because, truthfully, we deceive ourselves into thinking that we are safe only behind those walls. No one can get to us and, consequently, no one can hurt us. However, another by-product of these walls is that they often give the outside world the idea that we are strong, self-assured, well-adjusted individuals who don't need anyone else. That's the vibe we give off, and the world tells us it's a good vibe, a good way to be.

I'm here to tell you that the result is actually loneliness. When you build a wall that shows strength and independence to the world, you end up all alone behind that wall, and before you know it, you're depressed or angry or bitter. The lies that bind us are slippery lies. If you believe one, then before you know it, you will believe the next and then the next and then the next, and then you find yourself so deceived about so many things that the truth is just too elusive.

You buy the lie from the Devil that strength is a desirable attribute, so much so that you begin to look for that in yourself above everything else. Strength becomes the one thing you want to be known for. Unfortunately, that means you then have to be strong, which translates into handling things on your own. It's weak to ask for help, so you don't. You handle your problems, your family's problems; you handle it all. You might be the one others come to for help, but you don't ask for it in return. Because you're strong. That's your identity, and the world tells you that it is good.

What the Devil knows but you and I don't know about this seemingly desirable trait is that it will always lead to incapacitating loneliness. When you are handling everything, you are the only one to rely on. It's just you. So when life gets really weird and you get to the point that you're pretty sure you can't handle another thing, guess who you're left with? That's right—you. You're left with you, and God didn't create any of His children to live that way. He created us for community and to help one another.

He created man and saw that he was alone and then acknowledged that it wasn't good. God said that man's being alone was bad not because man needed a pretty lady, but because man needed community. Man was not created to be alone, so doesn't it make sense that the Devil would use the lie that strength in self is attractive and desirable and must be sought after? It does make sense because believing that lie will ultimately lead to our being alone—one thing we were not created to be.

The Bible is full of references that speak to the fact that God's children are to be in community together. We are to belong to a local church, helping each other and being helped by each other. That is a commandment. Hebrews 10:24-25 says,

And let us consider how to stir up one another to love and good works, not neglecting to meet together, as is the habit of some, but encouraging one another, and all the more as you see the Day drawing near.

You and I should make a habit of church attendance and thus share strength with our brothers and sisters in Jesus Christ. We often can avoid loneliness if we do.

However, what if we've already created a situation where we've shut everyone out because of our sin? Or what if because of our sin we've been shut out by others and we find ourselves alone? What if because of circumstances and the consequences of sin, we are alone, and now we are simply lost in the despair of that loneliness? What do we do then?

I feel compelled to speak the truth about the reality of those situations because I've lived through them and because I have family members who are living in that despair right now, even as I write. Because of the weight of their own sin and the struggles they've encountered while trying to get out from under that sin, they've convinced themselves that they have no choice but to be alone. However, that life will always lead to the despair of loneliness, and then the cycle continues. "I've got to be alone because of my sin, but I'm so lonely that I'm in despair."

It breaks my heart to watch those I love hurt, but it also breaks my heart because I've been there. And the core lie has always been, "Be strong. You can handle this on your own. No one else will understand." Then you're left to face the consequences alone.

The truth is, however, that my family member isn't alone, just as I wasn't. Not ever. This member of my family knows the Lord. He is a child of the Most High, the beloved of the Holy Bridegroom, just as I was in the midst of my darkest times. I can confidently write this truth that is a truth for all Christians: you are never alone. Never.

After my final affair came out, I was trying to put the pieces of my broken life back together in the weeks following. I had created such a persona of strength and self-sufficiency over the years that when the walls came crashing down, I had no one. I'd spent my life building those walls, but now that they were down and I was left exposed, I was alone. I felt like I was drowning in that loneliness, because even though I was falling apart, life was still going on. I was still teaching, and my children were still playing football and baseball and needing help with their homework. Laundry still needed to be done and grocery shopping completed. I truly felt like I would be crushed under the weight of my own self-imposed loneliness, so one day I did something that had become fairly common for me.

I made sure the boys were set up downstairs doing something, and I went up to my walk-in closet, closed the door, and sobbed. That closet had become the only place I could really let go and be in despair since I definitely didn't want my boys to see. I'd put them through enough already. I figured the last thing they needed to see was their mommy falling apart... again. So I went into my closet, shut the door, and screamed into a pillow. I cried out to God, "Where are You? I'm so alone! You promised that You wouldn't leave me, but I can't feel you! Where are You?!" I wept and wept, and then, just as my Father has done for me many times before, He filled my head with an image.

In this image, I could see myself lying in the fetal position in the middle of what looked like a large, endless desert. And in that image I was doing exactly what I was doing in that closet: crying alone. The image seemed to confirm the way I saw my existence, and it made me cry even harder; the despair was almost unbearable.

Just then, the image began to change. It was still me, curled up in that vast desert-like place, but the image began to pan out. I grew smaller and smaller, but I could see more and more of what was around me. Eventually the image panned out far enough so that I could see that I was in the fetal position and I was alone, but I wasn't in a desert. I was curled up in a tight ball right in the middle of a great big hand. My head was instantly filled with these words:

You are not alone, Debbie. I am there in the closet with you. I am holding you. I will always be with you, holding you, and I will never let you go.

That, my friends, is truth. Our Father does not promise us a rose garden while we are here on this earth. Often the toxic dump of a life we live in is because we've caused it or it's been caused by others, but for God's children, we are never alone in it. Don't let the Devil convince you that your strength is your shield. It is Jesus who shields us, protects us, and loves us. Your self-sufficiency may get you accolades from the world for a short period of time, but it will leave you empty and completely alone. It may seem that the only course of action is to shut yourself away from the rest of the world because of who you are, but that loneliness will take you to despair.

Instead, hang onto this truth: He is in that apartment with you. He is in that bed with you, in that closet with you, in that jail cell with you. He is with you. And He promises that He will never, ever leave you. You are not alone. Don't believe the lie and live as if you are.

YOU ARE FELLOW HEIRS WITH CHRIST

Like I've said before, the Devil's most successful deceptions are those that are almost true, the ones that start out with a little truth in them. Then he skews that truth just slightly, and it goes haywire.

Think about a compass. Let's suppose you are told to head due north, but your compass isn't true. The compass you're following is off by only a tenth of a degree. You won't notice that you are heading in the wrong direction at first. As a matter of fact, your route will look exactly as it should for a little while. However, that tenth of a degree means that you are systematically moving slightly off-course. At first, you don't notice because the variation is so slight, but it becomes apparent eventually. By then, you've traveled miles in the wrong direction. That's the tactic the Devil often uses with Christians so that he can make them follow a lie. So it is when we contemplate what we deserve for our sins and what we have actually received.

There are two truths at play here. The first truth is the one that the Devil won't shy from, and that's the truth of what we deserve. No matter who we are, if we have sinned, then we deserve death. The Bible is clear on that. Romans 3:23 says, *For the wages of sin is death.*

Wages are earned. When you perform a job, you receive the agreed upon wages in relation to the work you've completed. You aren't *given* wages without earning them. That's exactly why Paul uses the word "wages" here in regard to sin. What we earn because we sin is death. And everyone sins. No one is perfect. The only perfect Man who ever lived was the One who paid what you owe.

You see, the payment that was made on the cross is the truth that the Devil wants to keep from you. When the partial truth that you deserve every horrible thing that happens to you as a result of your sin is thrown at you while you are still in the middle of your sin, you can get lost in despair.

However, a partial truth becomes a lie when it is left incomplete. It becomes a lie because it leaves the hearer following a compass that no longer points true north, so the hearer will draw conclusions that will lead away from truth, not toward it. Romans 6:23 gives the entire truth. It's important that the compass you follow correctly indicates true north. The entirety of that passage says,

For the wages of sin is death, but the free gift of God is eternal life in Christ Jesus our Lord.

The culmination of this truth is that a believer will not receive what he or she has earned because God gives eternal life as a gift, no strings attached, and that gift is possible because the debt was instead paid by God's Son, Jesus Christ. But there is more, and the more is the truth you must cling to when the Devil tries to give you partial truths and lies.

Later in the book of Romans, Paul goes on to tell us more about this free gift and what believers will really receive instead of what they deserve. Romans 8:14-18 reads,

For all who are led by the Spirit of God are sons of God. For you did not receive the spirit of slavery to fall back into fear, but you have received the Spirit of adoption as sons, by whom we cry, "Abba! Father!" The Spirit himself bears witness with our spirit that we are children of God, and if children, then heirs—heirs of God and fellow heirs with Christ, provided we suffer with him in order that we may also be glorified with him.

Paul gives us the truth of what we receive, and it is glorious! First, he says that we do not have to worry that we will lose what we have been given because we have been adopted by God as His sons and daughters. That's tremendously good news, especially for those of us whose lives were characterized by the sin we committed in our false identities.

Paul says we no longer have to fear that we might get what we deserve. Instead, when we have those feelings, we can cry, "Abba! Father!" The term "Abba" used here by Paul was also used by Jesus to refer to God as Father. "Abba" is an intimate rendering of the term for "Father," some even defining it more like "Daddy" in modern English. In other words, when fear of getting what we deserve for our sin invades our hearts, as adopted children of God we can cry out to Him as our Daddy, the intimate Father and protector of His children. We have that kind of relationship with the Creator of the universe. Like I said, it's glorious.

Next, Paul tells us that in our relationship as God's children, we are also heirs. But heirs to what? Paul says we are "heirs of God" and "fellow heirs with Christ." It is vitally important that we understand what that means so that we can rest in our true identity, our true destiny in the middle of this sometimes difficult life.

Now that we are children of God, we are heirs of God, which literally means we inherit God. We will live in eternity actually being in His presence, experiencing every magnificent facet of His existence forever and ever. Revelation 21:3 describes it like this:

Behold, the dwelling place of God is with man. He will dwell with them, and they will be his people, and God himself will be with them as their God.

What a wonderful and awe-inspiring inheritance we have received. We will inherit God Himself! We will live forever with God, and He with us! We deserve death and the wrath of the very God who instead provided a way for us not only to have our debts paid, but to have Him as our very own! This is the truth upon which we must live.

And this really should be enough, right? I mean, inheriting the very God of all creation should be enough, but our Abba Father is extravagant in His gift-giving, especially when it comes to bestowing gifts on His beloved children. Paul also says that we are "fellow heirs with Christ." That means that we will receive the same inheritance as Jesus, sharing in what is His. That inheritance is the earth and all that is in it. It is eternity as co-heirs and

117

co-rulers with our Savior, who gladly shares what is rightfully His, even sacrificing Himself so that He might do so, all because the love of the Father and the love of the Son is based on their character and not on ours.

Therefore, you and I can rest in this lifetime, knowing that we will truly escape what we deserve, but not because we did anything to eliminate receiving that wage. No, we have been adopted into the family of God, and we are now His children. Since this is true, we have inherited both God and all that He has given to His Son, sharing that with our Savior and Lord.

I am convinced that if we were eternally-minded enough to move past the darkness of this world and to look toward what has been promised to us as the children of the Most High, then the lies and half-truths that the Devil tries to throw our way would not derail us. Instead, these promises would propel us toward proclaiming the life-giving truths we know.

Do you want truth? Here it is: as a believer, you are an heir to eternity with Jesus Christ. How awesome!

AS FAR AS THE EAST IS FROM THE WEST

About two years after my last affair came out, two years down the road toward truth, I was on my way to pick my boys up from school. I was listening to Christian radio, and I remember that I was once again lost in the regret of my past sins. Every time I thought about all of the horrible things I'd done over the course of my life, my thoughts would go back to regret and pain and guilt. While some measure of remembrance is absolutely necessary when it comes to the forgiveness we've received, living in bondage to the memories is just another lie the Devil tells us so that we will remain immobile in our lives.

It took me a long time to get past the lie that it was too late, that I'd finally sinned too grievously or too many times to be forgiven. I was beginning to lay hold of the truth that there is no "too late" for God's children because God will always forgive His children when they ask for forgiveness. However, Satan's bag of tricks is quite deep, and the lie that usually replaces the one that says you are too far gone for forgiveness is the lie of condemnation. This lie keeps your sins ever at the forefront of your mind, not so that you can remember how great your Redeemer is, but to bind you to the guilt of what you did despite the generosity of that Redeemer.

The guilt of past sins was still tormenting me, and this particular day was no exception. Once again the Devil had taken a truth and tweaked it a hair so that it became a bondage. I was driving and crying out to God in pain and regret, "Please forgive me, Father. I'm so sorry for the things I've done, for the pain I've caused my family and my friends. Thank you for loving me, even though I have done nothing but prove how unlovable I actually am."

As I was crying, I realized that a song I had never heard before was playing on the radio. The name of the song was "What Sin" by Morgan Cryar. It was an old song, but still I had never heard it. As I listened to the first verse, I was lost in the same pain as that expressed by the singer, and I cried with him. The verse goes like this:

> "It happened so long ago
> And I cried out for mercy back then
> I plead the blood of Jesus
> Begged him to forgive my sin
> But I still can't forget it
> It just won't go away
> So I wept again, "Lord, wash my sin,"

As I listened to the words of this song, I couldn't stop the tears. "Yes, Father, that's exactly my prayer," I cried aloud. "Please wash away my sin. I'm so sorry." And then the song continued,

"But this is all He'd say,

What sin, what sin?
Well, that's as far away
as the east is from the west
What sin, what sin?
It was gone the very minute you confessed
Buried in the sea of forgetfulness."

Suddenly my tears stopped. I listened with new attentiveness, faced with yet another truth the Enemy had tried hard to keep from me. Verse two went on:

"The heaviest thing you'll carry
Is a load of guilt and shame
You were never meant to bear them
So let them go in Jesus name
Our God is slow to anger
Quick to forgive our sin
So let Him put them under the blood
Don't bring them up again
Cause He'll just say,

"What sin, what sin?
Well, that's as far away
as the east is from the west
What sin, what sin?
It was gone the very minute you confessed
Buried in the sea of forgetfulness." [1]

As we know, our souls are secure in eternity the moment we accept the glorious gift of salvation from our Lord Jesus Christ, so there is absolutely nothing the Devil can do to have us. However, what he can do and does at every chance he gets is to lie to us, hoping that in believing those lies, we will become frozen in our own guilt, despair, loneliness, or hopelessness. Another of his favorite lies—that God will not forgive—has deceived so many wonderful men and women, and it's generally so successful because we honestly can't fathom this level of forgiveness.

The song, "What Sin," was based on a beautiful psalm of David, Psalm 103:10-12,

He does not deal with us according to our sins, nor repay us according to our iniquities. For as high as the heavens are above the earth, so great is his steadfast love toward those who fear him; as far as the east is from the west, so far does he remove our transgressions from us.

It is important to note that David doesn't say, "As far as the north is from the south," because that is a finite distance. "As far as the east is from the west," however, is infinite. When God forgives us, He literally casts our sins from His presence. The Devil would have us hold onto them, feeling

[1]*"What Sin,"* by Morgan Cryar, from the album, Love on Fire, 1995

the pain and remorse that immobilizes us continually, but David reminds us that God has cast them from His sight. That's the truth we must cling to, even as we remember those sins so that we are thankful to the God who forgave.

The truths that you and I are to hold onto are eternal truths, and in order to hang onto them, we must be eternally minded. This world is not our home, but we are here in this time and in this place on purpose. The Creator of heaven and earth is building our stories, so that like Job, David, Esther, Ruth, and the millions of other men and women God uses to advance His kingdom, we, too, might be used to let a dying world know the only Savior who can bring them from darkness into eternal light.

You are valuable. You are a reflection of Christ. You are never alone. You are heirs to eternity and fellow heirs with Christ. And you are a new creation in Jesus; the old has passed away, and the new has come. Stand in the truth of who you are—of Whose you are—and break the chains of deception and identity-lies the Devil would tell you to keep you from those glorious truths. God trusts you, He loves you, and He will use you to the advancement of His kingdom. You need only walk in the truth of your identity in Christ.

May the God of all creation, El Shaddai, Jehovah Nissi, Jehovah Shalom, keep you and show you all measure of truth and kindness as you move in this world, waiting on the glorious day of your inheritance with all the saints in glory. Amen.

WHAT IF I DON'T KNOW JESUS?

Some of you may be reading this book because you are bound by your past, maybe even your present, and you picked it up hoping it would help. The problem is that some of you may not know Jesus as your Savior. The bad news is that the hope presented in this book isn't for you, and that is really bad news. But the good news is tremendously good because this hope can be yours.

Without Christ, there is truly no hope for breaking the chains that prompted you to read this book in the first place. Every living person who does not know the power and life of Jesus as Lord is in chains to a hopeless existence and the lies of the Devil, whether they acknowledge those chains or not. There is an old saying that everyone believes in Jesus as Savior—if not in this life, then one millisecond after they take their last breath.

Let's make reading this book about good news. If you want the freedom I've written about in these few pages, if you want to know the peace and security that is eternal, then there is no time like now.

All of us have sinned. The Bible says, "For all have sinned and fall short of the glory of God" (Romans 3:23). The Bible also tells us that the debt we owe for our sin is death, "For the wages of sin is death..." (Romans 6:23). However, God knew we were sinners who deserved that penalty, and so did Jesus, and they both loved us too much to leave us like that. Therefore, our Heavenly Father provided a way so that His perfect justice could remain, but we might still live. "But God shows his love for us in that while we were still sinners, Christ died for us" (Romans 5:8). In other words, Jesus came and lived a perfect life and then gave that life in death as payment for our sins. He paid our debt.

Would you like to know how you can receive that gift? It really is easy, but it must be genuine. The Bible tells us how. "If you confess with your mouth that Jesus is Lord and believe in your heart that God raised him from the dead, you will be saved. For with the heart one believes and is justified, and with the mouth one confesses and is saved" (Romans 10:9-10). If you are ready right now to make the truths of this book and the beauties of being a forever child of God yours, then pray this prayer:

Dear God,
I believe what You say is true. I believe that Jesus is Your Son, and I believe
that You sent Him down to earth to give His life in payment for my sins. I
believe that He is Your Son, the Son of God, and I believe that the grave
couldn't hold Him because He is Your Son. I believe that He was resurrected
after three days and that He lives now in heaven with You. I accept all of
these things as true, and I want Jesus to be my Savior. I accept His gift on
my behalf so that I, too, can live forever with You in eternal joy and peace.
Thank You for this amazing gift, and thank you, Jesus, for dying
on the cross so that I could live.

From this moment forward, I am a child of God and
Jesus is my Lord and my Savior.
Amen.

That's it. If you prayed that prayer and if you truly believe all that you just said, then be assured, you are saved. You are a new creation. The Bible assures us, "For everyone who calls on the name of the Lord will be saved" (Romans 10:13). God heard you, and now you are His! That means all the joy, all the promises, and all the treasure that are spoken about in Scripture are yours.

If you don't have a Bible, you will want to obtain one as soon as you can. Many local churches will provide one at no charge, or there are unfortunately plenty available at secondhand bookstores. The next thing to do is to go to church. Learn about this Jesus who saved you. The more you know of Him, the more you will want to know. This is a wonderful day for you, my friend. A wonderful, eternally-perfect day.

I'm so happy for you! Congratulations, and if I don't get to meet you in this life, I'll see you in heaven!

One Woman,
One Business at a Time

ABOUT THE AUTHOR

Dr. Deb currently lives in Tucson, Arizona, with her husband of thirty-two years, Jeff, and their two dogs, Levi and Hattie. She has two adult sons, Spence and Miles, both of whom are steadily moving toward God's work in their own lives. Dr. Deb is the President and CEO of Love Everlasting Ministries, an international women's ministry dedicated to breaking barriers of isolation for women everywhere through education, study, and connection to one another in the body of Christ.

Her latest project is a school for widows and impoverished women called the Reap What You Sew Project. It is a tailoring school set to launch in Blantyre, Malawi, this year. This school will offer six months of training in the trade of tailoring, as well as two weeks of business training. At the end of the six months, each qualifying student will receive the sewing machine she has been sewing on, as well as enough cloth and other materials to begin her own tailoring business. By helping women provide for themselves and their children, Dr. Deb says that, "We will help change women, their children, their villages, and finally, their nations." For more information on how you can be involved in sponsoring this school, as well as being personally connected to one of the students, please visit loveeverlastingministries.com today.

Dr. Deb is available for conferences, book signings, and retreats. Simply contact her on her website, DebWaterbury.com, where you can email her and also see her other books, podcasts, blogs, and messages available for purchase or download.

Softball, 1974

7th Grade
school picture

My new look, 1976

My church, 1974

Senior picture, 1981

Senior Prom, 1980

Wedding day,
1985

Homecoming, 1980

*Pregnant
with Spence,
1986*

*Vacation
Bible School,
Georgia,
1987*

*Deb, Spence and
Miles at the
Grand Canyon, 1994*

Jeff with his F-4 fighter jet, 1991

Deb with Spence, 1986

Waterburys in Hawaii, 1991

*Deb and Jeff F-16
taxi ride, 2016*

*Deb, Miles and
Spence, Christmas in
New York, 2016*

lovetruthlive

WITH DEB WATERBURY

Teaching that the love of Christ
and the Truth of Scripture lead
to life-changing freedom

*"By this all people will
know that you are my
disciples, if you have
love for one another."*
– John 13:35

debwaterbury.com

lovetruthlive

WITH DEB WATERBURY

PAINTED WINDOW TRILOGY:
Painted Window, Threads and White Zephyr

Follow Elizabeth Percy's allegorical
journey into discovering the love
that transforms all of our lives –
the love of Jesus, our Bridegroom.

James on the Mount

A study of the book of James as it relates
to the Sermon on the Mount.

DAILY DEVOTIONAL SERIES:

Bible devotional studies, verse by verse.

- *Galatians* (3 month devotional)
- *Ephesians* (3 month devotional)
- *Philippians* (3 month devotional)

WOMEN'S MINISTRY STUDIES:

6 Pairs of Sandals
Yesterday's Footsteps and Today's
Women's Ministry

ADDITIONAL RESOURCES AT

www.debwaterbury.com

Dr. Deb Waterbury
also offers:
Windows of the Heart Podcast Teachings
(also available through iTunes)
and
Voices of Love Blogs

Visit us on Facebook, Twitter, Instagram,
LinkedIn, Pinterest and YouTube

Note:
*Dr. Deb Waterbury continues to expand
her resource catalogue, so please log onto
her website for the most recent additions.*